Library of
Davidson College

THE PROSTITUTE IN PROGRESSIVE LITERATURE

The Prostitute in Progressive Literature
Khalid Kishtainy

Allison & Busby
London/New York

First published in 1982 by
Allison and Busby Limited
6a Noel Street, London W1V 3RB, England
and distributed in the USA by
Schocken Books Inc.
200 Madison Avenue, New York, N.Y. 10016

Copyright © 1982 by Khalid Kishtainy

British Library Cataloguing in Publication Data:

Kishtainy, Khalid
   The prostitute in progressive literature.
   1. Prostitution in literature
   I. Title
   809'.933'53   PN56.P/

ISBN 0-85031-439-9

Photoset in 10/11 Baskerville by
Derek Doyle & Associates, Mold, Clwyd
and printed in Great Britain by
Biddles Ltd., Guildford & King's Lynn.

Contents

	Introduction	7
1	Prostitution in History and Literature	13
2	Under the Shadow of Capitalism	27
3	Victims of Circumstance	41
4	Brecht and his Underworld	52
5	Under Colonialism	63
6	Black Women, White Men	74
7	The Woman with the Heart of Gold	85
8	The Eternal Shadow of the Warrior	99
9	The Avenger and her Problem	108
10	Redemption	119
	Notes	133
	Index	138

(By kind permission of the Iraqi Cultural Centre, London.)

The first known representation in history of a prostitute: a Babylonian statue of the temple harlot mentioned in the *Epic of Gilgamesh*, 1700 BC, the earliest epic poem. In its bold realism, the figurine stands apart from the rest of ancient Mesopotamian sculpture.

Introduction

The mysteries of death and sex, the act of regeneration and new life, have occupied people's minds ever since they found spare time for thought free from the hand-to-mouth pursuit of food. The result was the emergence of two categories of those exempted from the production operations of society, namely the artists and the prophets. While the artist expanded the mental horizon of death and sex to the realms of pathos and love, the prophet ritualized them to the smallest detail. With the improved methods of feeding the community, more leisure was accumulated to indulge in activities which were scarcely related to production. Sex for sex's sake became the rule rather than the exception. The biological and instinctive peculiarities of man and woman, the economic domination of man, the precarious equilibrium of man-made society and a host of other minor factors produced the casual act of sex procured by man from woman for a consideration.

Thus evolved, prostitution became a new preoccupation for both the artist and the prophet. With the rise of Judaism and its enlarged superego, man's second oldest profession, to borrow the title of B.L. Reitman's book on prostitution, became the symbol for all the evil that could hit the community. The influence which Judaism had on the followers of monotheism, the Christians and Muslims, made that conception nearly universal. From Isaiah and Hosea to Shakespeare and Zola, the whore and the son of the whore were projected as targets of contempt, fear or compassion.

A drastic change of attitude took place during the nineteenth century, when modern thinkers began to re-examine all the conclusions and beliefs of the past generations. It happened that while those pioneers of our present-day thought were busy on their inquiries, capitalism brought prostitution to a stage beyond anything hitherto known in history. It was natural for this phenomenon to command the primary attention of researchers and social thinkers. The commitment to society felt by most serious

European writers introduced the subject here and there into the fiction and drama of the period. The harlot lurked in the dark corners of their back streets, over their bridges of sighs and their embankment suicide scenes. She languished in prisons and lay, disease-ridden, gasping her last breath as a victim or a sacrifice. She even took full command of the plot and became the author's heroine and centre of attention.

The driving force for a great number of artists and idealists, or all of them as the Freudians may insist, has been the inner psycho-neurotic conflict which found a solution or an outlet in their works of art or social crusades. In previous civilizations, this form of resolution of the inner conflict through artistic expression was given indirect idealistic themes. In our own modern times, the sense of freedom and the triumph of sexology over conventionalism opened the doors for the same category of subliminationists to come out and express themselves more directly. The depressive horror of the flesh, the manic thirst for sex, guilt-burdened idealism and any number of other psychological complexes introduced the prostitute into the creative work of our modern artists as a versatile medium for self-expression.

Out of the misery of Europe's proletarian masses rose the flame of socialism, and out of socialist thought sprang up the banner of revolt and revolution. The numerous poets, dramatists and novelists who advocated social change spoke with great emphasis on moralization. Whether endowed with a heart of gold or a kiss of poison and disease, the harlot has always occupied a dominant position in the mind of the moralists. Like the prophets of the Bible, who equated harlotry with the corruption of heathenism, the modern prophets of *Das Kapital* equated prostitution with the exploitation of capitalism – but with a difference. The difference here is that the Hebrew prophets threw out the baby with the bathwater and stamped the prostitute and her profession as forces of evil, whereas the progressive writers of our era differentiated between the two.

To the socialists, the female prostitute represented all the evils that have been brought about or multiplied by the capitalists. She represented the enslavement of women by men and the exploitation of workers by the capitalist crooks; the common front of the unholy alliance of church, police and finance was found best exemplified in the common position taken by this front towards the prostitute; brotheldom provided the natural setting for the broken homes, lonely women, parentless children and general decadence, bestiality and corruption associated with bourgeois industrial life. The seduction and ruthless destruction of the poor by the rich invoked the familiar stories of the hapless peasant girl employed as a chambermaid, seduced, made pregnant and expelled. The devastation of modern wars aroused the imagination of the writer with their trail of widowed and abandoned women, orphaned girls and exposed females all gradually drifting into prostitution. In these wars women of the defeated nations and colonial world could find no better option but to submit to the bayonets of the conquerors and look for a living in the cafés and nightclubs frequented by soldiers. The predominance of immigrants and minorities among the brothel population underlined the prejudiced exploitation of the minorities. All these evils were the targets of committed writers and they were all present in prostitution.

The concept of waste which happened to be so much of the stuff of Shakespearian tragedy, and likewise the backbone of the socialist critique, was also evidenced in its starkest form in the career of prostitution, the dissipation of women's youth and men's energy and health, the loss of aborted babies, the squandering of daily wages and the easy use of prostitution-earned money, the waste of time, talent, love and care, and in the very waste of the unsatisfying mechanical coitus itself.

Characteristically enough, the revolutionaries, marxists and radical thinkers had scarcely dealt with the problem of prostitution in depth. Unlike the idealists and reformers of bourgeois thought, who occupied themselves with the question to the point of obsession – as in the case of Gladstone – they treated it as a mere symbol, a figure of speech or an example for illustration in their heated discussions on the nature and future of capitalism. To them, the problem was a very simple one caused by economic needs and destined to disappear with the abolition of poverty. The prostitute was therefore left to the artists and writers who had the time, scope and artistic means to blow the examples and metaphors of their ideological mentors into a size larger than life.

Nearly every progressive dramatist or story writer thought at one stage or another of the prostitute as a character worthy of artistic treatment. The more restive and furious at the conditions of society the writer was, the stronger that writer felt the pull towards the subject. The essence of such fury may be grasped in the frequent loss of control over the subject matter, and over the plausible depiction of the whore, by many writers noted otherwise for their realism – like Emile Zola. Another more recent example may be cited in *Jesus as Seen by his Friends*, the play by the left-wing Israeli writer Amos Kenan which was banned by the Israeli censor. With Mary turned into a whore and Jesus into a pimp, the writer could find no better theme to crown his habitual indictment of the Zionist establishment and its society.

It does not surprise me now that the first adventure in writing that I personally made during my university years – the years of student idealism, high-pitched anti-imperialist struggle and dedication to the cause of the socialist revolution in Iraq – was a play about a prostitute who couldn't understand why she was not allowed to dispose of her baby as she wanted. In the early 1950s, the old brothel ghetto of Baghdad, the historic Kallachia, became the haunt of the revolutionary intellectuals who frequented the place almost as a patriotic duty and often without having so much as the money to pay, the confidence to approach a pimp or the guts to come anywhere near any woman. We used to stroll into the nooks and crannies of the old lanes, reciting passages from the *Communist Manifesto* and verses from Bahr al-Ulum's poem on the prostitute's grave. There was the painter who paid a black whore only to sit for him. There was the story writer who invited a blind one to a meal of kebab only to hear her story. There was the art critic who went as far as buying himself a rubber sheath only to end up by inflating it into a balloon. There was the real political writer who actually went to bed with Zahra and came out crying.

Needless to say, neither my play nor any of the creations of my friends came to anything. Yet it is peculiar that years after that period I find myself once more drawn to the subject. The fire of the artist and the faith of the idealist have given way to the detachment and scepticism of the disillusioned. The creative impulse which should have added another item, however small and mediocre, to the wealth of literature of revolt is replaced by the observant eye which could only survey what others have done.

Undoubtedly, my experiences and thoughts were, and are, shared by masses of people in so many places where the struggle against idiotic conditions is at its sharpest. In the concluding chapters of *The Idiot*, Dostoevsky related how the intelligentsia of his time were expected to forego their real love for the women of their hearts and embrace fallen women for no other reason than proving their point vis-à-vis the "woman question", that "a fallen woman was, indeed, superior to a woman who had not fallen". Wherever there is inequality, there is enslavement of women and exploitation and degeneration of sex. Therefore the subject of prostitution to the sociologist is like the subject of the atom to the physicist or anatomy to the physiologist.

One of the annoying points in this question is that we have become so used to viewing it from the Judeo-Christian angle of tradition that we can scarcely imagine any other angle from which one can have a different look. The Judeo-Christian view represented in reality only a fraction of the human race and its history, and although we find that all the writers whom we have to examine reflect its influence, a brief look at the different points of view which were once just as universal and normal is nevertheless useful.

The definition of "prostitute" and prostitution is a difficult one and a question over which the legislators of many lands and nations differed. Even more perplexing is the definition of who is "progressive" and who is not. Perhaps the wiser approach, or at least more practical, is to avoid such hair-splitting disputation and leave people to their own taste. This book, therefore, does not confine itself to any category and deals with a wide spectrum of writers who looked at the prostitute in terms of a social problem rather than an individual sinner. Please don't ask what makes me take that as a mark of "progressiveness".

Most of the literature discussed in the present work was written at a time when religion, Victorian morality and male chauvinism reigned supreme. Concepts like "fallen women" and "female purity" may seem as incomprehensible and objectionable to our permissive society as our acceptance of unmarried mothers and liberated feminism would have seemed to our fathers. One cannot over-emphasize the need to bear this point in mind while reading this book. The sociological and historical discussions are included mainly for the purpose of establishing the proper background and social milieu against which the writers, thinkers and artists of the period operated.

1

Prostitution in History and Literature

The obsession of artists with prostitution and sex in general is quite remarkable and has a long history behind it. One of the earliest documents in the possession of the British Museum is a papyrus letter written by an Egyptian mother to her husband complaining to him about a group of sculptors who descended on the village to carry out some work and corrupted the young female inhabitants in the process.

The Sumerian *Epic of Gilgamesh*, whose hero is the king of Uruk in ancient Mesopotamia, is the earliest record of the interest shown by poets and story-tellers in the character of the prostitute. Tablets containing parts of the epic were first unearthed by Austen Henry Layard in the first half of the nineteenth century. The full significance of the discovery was related by George Smith to the Society of Biblical Archaeology in 1872 and the poem is generally accepted as dating from the early centuries of the third millennium BC. It is assumed, however, that the story had been in circulation a few centuries earlier. Although the story had been in circulation some five thousand years ago, its theme and ideas, strangely enough, have remained valid till the present day and have echoed many of the attitudes of our contemporary writers.

The epic tells the story of King Gilgamesh and his companion Enkidu, a savage man who was reared on the milk of the beasts and ate grass with the gazelle of the wilderness. He was as strong as a star from heaven, and his presence thwarted the hunters of Uruk and moved them to find ways of getting rid of him. They commissioned a harlot, a wanton from the temple of love, to use her woman's power to overpower this man. The harlot went and lay in wait for Enkidu at the well where he drank. As he came with the wild creatures of the plains, the harlot made her breasts bare, uncovered her nakedness and welcomed his eagerness.

As he lay on her murmuring love, she taught him the woman's

art. For six days and seven nights they lay together, for Enkidu had forgotten his home in the hills; but when he was satisfied he went back to the wild beasts. Then, when the gazelle saw him, they bolted away; when the wild creatures saw him they fled. Enkidu would have followed, but his body was bound as though with a cord, his knees gave way when he started to run, his swiftness was gone. And now the wild creatures had all fled away; Enkidu was grown weak, for wisdom was in him, and the thoughts of a man were in his heart.

The harlot led Enkidu into the city of Uruk, where she taught him the ways of civilization. She divided her clothes in two and with one half she dressed him; she taught him to eat baked bread and drink strong wine. "He became merry, his heart exulted and his face shone. He rubbed down the matted hair of his body and anointed himself with oil. Enkidu had become a man; but when he had put on man's clothing, he appeared like a bridegroom."

The savage was tamed by the harlot, only to discover after a while the price of civilization. Stricken with disease, he cursed from his deathbed the harlot who had brought him to this:

> With a great curse I curse you! I will promise you a destiny to all eternity. My curse shall come on you soon and sudden. You shall be without a roof for your commerce, for you shall not keep house with other girls in the tavern, but do your business in places fouled by the vomit of the drunkard. Your hire will be potter's earth, your thievings will be flung into the hovel, you will sit at the crossroads in the dust of the potter's quarter, you will make your bed on the dunghill at night, and by day take your stand in the wall's shadow. Brambles and thorns will tear your feet, the drunk and the dry will strike your cheek and your mouth will ache.

For all intents and purposes, Enkidu's curse seems to have been fulfilled to all eternity. But, strangely enough, the writer of the *Epic* thought out such a destiny at a time when prostitution was a form of worship and the harlot a part of the Temple hierarchy. However, Shamash, the wise god of the city, disapproved of Enkidu's curse:

> Enkidu, why are you cursing the woman, the mistress who taught you to eat bread fit for gods and drink wine of kings? She who put upon you a magnificent garment, did she not give you glorious Gilgamesh for your companion, and has not Gilgamesh, your own brother, made you rest on a royal bed and recline on a couch at his left hand?

When Enkidu heard these words, he changed his mind and recalled that curse:

> Woman, I promise you another destiny. The mouth which cursed you shall bless you. Kings, princes and nobles shall adore you. On your account a man though twelve miles off will clap his hands to his thigh and his hair will twitch. For you he will undo his belt and open his treasure and you shall have your desire; lapis lazuli, gold and cornelian from the heap of the treasury. A ring for your hand and a robe shall be yours. The priest will lead you into the presence of the gods. On your account a wife, a mother of seven, was forsaken.

This prayer seems also to have been fulfilled. The writer of the Sumerian poem had foreshadowed the ambivalence which has marked our intellectual attitudes to the prostitute in modern times. On the one hand, she is presented with misgivings as the symbol of decay, the corruption of purity and the dissipation of manhood and strength; on the other, she is idealized as the woman with the golden heart, the instrument of civilization and the sacrificial lamb of the existing order. The Mesopotamian poet was conscious of both sides of the coin and responded to the morality of his age, which had institutionalized whoredom as an acceptable part of society, by blessing the wanton heroine of his epic. She is the woman who tamed the savage into a civilized being and turned the enemy of society and the scourge of the shepherds and hunters into a protector of their herds and champion of their city.

The poem came into circulation during the proto-literate phase of early Sumerian civilization some five thousand years ago. That was the time when men were occupied with the task of transforming barbarism into organized state and civilization. In the duel between the wild Enkidu and the king of the city, and the triumph of the latter over the former, the epic signalled the victory of urban life over primitive chaos. In this process, the prostitute played the role of the messenger of civilization, and the writer of the epic was truly the first progressive poet in the history of poetry.

In recognition of the function of the prostitute, the Babylonians and other ancient Semitic peoples of the Middle East called her *Qadishtu* or *q'deshah* (sacred) and institutionalized her profession within the temple. In this, the Semites were not alone. From Japan to the rocky mountains of the Red Indians, peoples accepted one form or another of prostitution (in the sense of promiscuous hiring of one's body for the sexual use of others) as a sacred, honourable or necessary part of the social organization based on private property.

More than one factor must have emerged to give rise to the

practice of prostitution so early in the history of man. The capture of women in warfare must have helped the process of adding the woman to the belongings of a man. The early division of labour which removed women from the direct task of hunting and fighting for food brought about the position wherein man received affection, care and sexual pleasure from the woman in exchange for food and commodities. The rise of private ownership initiated the whole apparatus of inheritance. The question of clear-cut succession became imperative and called for a jealously guarded fidelity on the part of the woman. This, in turn, called for a pool of women available for extra-marital pleasure. The greater the role of private ownership, the more the emphasis laid on the chastity of wives and on the organization of prostitution at the same time. Yet the emergence of prostitution seems doubtful without the instinctive and biological differences between the sexes.

The ruling classes of most nations evolved strict and often terrifying laws against the aggressor on this human property. So much so that in many societies, the penalty of death was imposed on the violation of chastity. Islam, for example, imposed the penalty of confinement until death, or flogging, on the adulterer and adulteress.[1] The more sophisticated societies removed the crudity of the passion of jealousy from the issue and stuck to strict commercial dealing involving compensation to be paid out to the aggrieved party on such grounds as seduction, breach of promise, criminal conversation, etc.

At the same time, we find throughout history the foundations of fidelity shaken, and free love on the increase, whenever the basis or value of private property is undermined. Hence the lax sexual morality of the poorer classes. The rise in fornication during and after wars and crisis is partly due to the uncertainty of the property market. During the Black Death when people began to leave their movable and immovable belongings behind and run to safer places, when entire families were carried off by death leaving no heirs whatsoever, sexual licence became the order of the day. Typical is the manner in which men used to leave their women behind as they did their chattels and cattle. A similar, albeit less apparent, development swept Germany in the Twenties with the fall of the German mark, as reflected in the literature of the expressionists and the plays of Brecht. The present outburst of sexual licence in the developed countries, for example, may conceivably have something to do with the unsettled money market, inflation and lack of interest in saving.

One may also observe that chastity disappeared or faded out in societies where private property had a very small role to play in the economic life of the community, as in the case of the Eskimos, the Muria community of India and some tribes in the Arabian peninsula. In societies where a communistic form of life was followed, as in Sparta, women became equal to men, and sexual taboos were hardly known. Prostitution in such communities made no sense and played no part, a discovery which became the basis of marxist thought on the problem of prostitution. The relation between this problem and economic inequality was in fact accepted by sociologists in general — as was expressed in the findings of the League of Nations, after its extensive study of the question, when it accepted that prostitution emerged whenever women fell below the economic and cultural status of men: "It appears to require for its existence a certain surplus of wealth and energy among at least one class of the population and to be favoured by an unequal distribution of wealth."[2]

As inequality was the rule in practically all societies, there was hardly any nation which lived without its whores. *Homo sapiens* is not a pairing species and sexual fidelity was a condition imposed on the members of society for the sake of the economic organization.[3] It rests, as do all unnatural things, on a precarious balance, a balance between the number of males and females, between the sexuality of the males and females and between the socio-economic powers of the two sexes and of the various classes. It is sufficient to remember the difference between the sexuality of man and woman to realize that such a balance is almost entirely impossible. Monogamous fidelity has never reigned comfortably, if at all, in most societies. Where the position of women was depressed and free love banished, women were forced to earn their bread by selling their bodies to men. This was achieved in the subtle and legal *harim* form of prostitution, the temporary marriage of *mut'a* (enjoyment) known in Islam, the religious temple harlotry of India and the ancient Middle East, or in the outright market dealing of European prostitution.

The close relationship between the property basis of the community and prostitution is projected in a different picture. The matriarchal society of ancient Egypt presents us with women who used to choose their own lovers. In the opinion of F. Henriques, male prostitution might have been the usual form which ancient Egyptian fornication assumed.[4] The increase of gigolos in the United States may also be a reflection on the position of women and the number of rich widows and divorcees. The only difference in prostitution between one property society and another has been one of quality, form and attitude. In the old kingdoms of the Middle East, where pleasure and fertility were the cult and guiding light of society, prostitution was treated as a respectable institution. In the temple of Mylitta in Assyria, women used to come and sit and wait for men to sleep with them for a silver coin thrown at them. At Heliopolis in Greece and Baalbek in Lebanon, virgin girls sat by the roadside waiting for strangers to come and deflower them before they got married. The same practice was followed in Armenia, where some of the women eventually made it their career while others confined themselves to a single act. In Cyprus, King Cinyras instituted sacred prostitution by installing Aphrodite, the daughter of the Salt Sea and Phallos, as the goddess of love to whom men gave a coin and enjoyed the pleasure of one of her harlots. The woman who, as a temple harlot, dedicated her life to the glory of god by providing sex for men became a familiar character in the towns and cities of the Middle East and India.

Such forms of respectable prostitution continued well into our own era. In Cyprus and Armenia, women prostituted themselves to collect a dowry as late as the eighteenth century. The women of Ouled Naïl (in Algeria), the island of Chios and parts of Japan and North America continued to do so with the approval of their societies. In the French Congo, women went out dancing in the villages, offering their virginity for a sum of money.[5]

Prostitution reached its highest level of artistry among the Greeks, whose love for the female body reached the point of devout worship. The story of Phryne, the charmer who won a legal case by overwhelming the jury with an exposure of her nude figure, is cited in many books.[6] Together with the worship of the female physique, sexual intercourse was to the Greeks a form of communion with God, as divorced from promiscuity as the Christian Holy Communion is from gluttony.[7] Sparta and Athens followed their different paths of collective life and individual enterprise. In Sparta, sex was made free for all and men used to encourage the healthy and strong youth to sleep with their women. A man might also seek the wife of another if he found her healthy and worth a pregnancy. To encourage such a successful natural selection, girls and boys were made to parade and compete in sport in the nude. All the offspring then belonged to the state. Prostitution had practically no role to play, and such women who gave all their time and preoccupation to provide sexual pleasure were called city workers.

On the other hand, the commercial life of Athens put women in a position similar to that of Victorian England and the French Second Empire. Wives were selected as part of the well-run enterprise of the man, economically calculated and scarcely related to love or sex.

Such things were reserved for the paid woman. The economic prosperity of the rich prompted Solon to legislate for prostitution and even made the state buy whores and cater for its citizens in the nationalized brothels (*dicteria*). The fees were truly made on a social service level, barely covering the expenses of the system. On the other hand, and significantly enough, the adulteress was punished with death. The brothel, however, was made a sanctuary in which men used to seek immunity from their creditors and wives.

The *dicteria* established schools of their own for the teaching of harlots. Out of such care and interest, the *hetaerae* appeared on the scene. The *hetaera* was a paid woman with an exceedingly impressive character, well endowed and educated and highly respected in society. Wherever men have accumulated great wealth and reached a sophisticated level, the ghost of the *hetaera* has roamed around. As much as she coloured the poetry of ancient Greece, she filled the novels and short stories of bourgeois France in the character of her successor, the courtesan. In Japan, where the attitude to sex is somewhat similar to that of Athens, the *hetaera* found a counterpart in the Geisha. China also produced such a respected class of professional paid women. The world of Islam had its Jaria and Qayna, the concubines of considerable poetic and musical accomplishments whose stories filled the Arabic classic *The Book of Songs*. The Islamic concubine, however, is more of a purchased slave than a freelance independent *hetaera*.

The position of women began to decline during the last stages of the Roman Empire. Unlike the Greek wives who remained faithful to their husbands and kept an orderly home for them, the rich wives of Rome joined in the orgy and even went out into the streets to practise prostitution. The promiscuity of the empire may best be summed up in Emperor Augustus's respectful reference to Horace as his (the Emperor's) "most immaculate penis". The male organ, which served for the Middle Eastern peoples as the symbol of fertility, was looked upon by the Romans as the symbol of power and energy. This, however, was by no means the cause of the increase in prostitution. The unprecedented dimensions of the empire which the Romans had created brought to Rome great numbers of slaves who offered the ready material for this profession. Wealth was accompanied, as usual, by the utter misery of the lower classes. The continuous wars fought on many fronts upset the natural equilibrium between the number of males and females and put the cream of Roman manhood out of circulation. The story of Anthony and Cleopatra and the poor wife sitting at home in Rome is a good example.

The unequal number of men and women meant that fewer men were available for marriage among the patrician class. In the *Satyricon*, Petronius left us with living pictures of what Roman fornication was like. The rich millionaire, Trimalchio, surrounded with wine, food and slaves, spoke of the wealth which he accumulated from selling wine and bacon, and recommended these words for his epitaph: "he rose from nothing and left thirty million. He never listened to a philosopher. God bless him." This was said while his stonemason was trying to make love to his lesbian wife in another corner of the chamber. In the story of the freed slave, we hear of a man living off the immoral earnings of Melissa, the publican's wife.[8]

The Romans hastened to organize the profession by legislation which provided for a register of harlots and described the manner in which the work should be done, the houses managed and taxes paid. Emperor Elagabalus (third century AD) made whoredom his particular state interest and opened a brothel in his own palace for his friends and slaves. On one occasion, he convened a meeting for the prostitutes in which he spoke and addressed them as "comrades" – an event which was never repeated until the establishment of the Soviet government and Lenin's attempt to reform the whores of tsarist Russia.

The fall of the harlot from her lofty position was effected by the rise of Judaism, which castigated the heathen temples and their *qadishas* (sacred harlots): "There shall be no whore of the daughters of Israel .... Thou shalt not bring the hire of a whore, or the price of a dog, into the house of the Lord."[9] The prophets went further and looked upon all manifestations of evil as synonymous with or derivative from whoredom. The generally accepted view is that the banishment of the whore was part of the new moral outlook of the Hebrews, an interpretation which itself calls for an interpretation, as it starts from the Judeo-Christian premise that prostitution is contrary to absolute morality. Nor can we easily accept the sounder suggestion that the Hebrews attacked whoredom as a manifestation of idolatry and a remnant of temple harlotry, the religion of their political foes. The Hebrews incorporated many heathen practices, including circumcision, ritual sacrifice and fetishism. The strict prohibition of prostitution was part of the banishment of the flesh and of sex associated with the development of Judaism and the teachings of the prophets during the eclipse of Hebrew rule in Palestine. The emphasis on chastity, prohibition of whoredom and adherence to the Decalogue were, according to Max Weber, late developments which took place in the post-exile era.[10]

The national catastrophes inflicted on the Jews activated a guilt complex and a depressive mood which found many expressions throughout the Old Testament and which emerged in such matters as the aversion to sex and flesh. The national peril throughout the kingdom had also called for more children to feed the war machine and for a tribal form of segregation which kept the blood pure. Both needs clashed with the practice of whoredom.

Whilst the moral teachings of Babylonia and Egypt revolved around the prudent enjoyment of life and sex,[11] the creed of the new monotheistic faith focused on the idea of prudence itself by being suspicious of sexual indulgence and physical exhibitionism,

Christ came to lift some of the depression by preaching forgiveness and love and giving a living example by associating himself with a harlot. Yet the tortuous development of Christianity did not spare it the old harassments and afflictions which had accompanied the growth of Judaism, and blocked up the window which Christ tried to open. The reduction of libido was even more intensified under the breath of the apostles and fathers of the church. St Paul ordered the Corinthians to deliver the fornicators unto Satan for the destruction of their flesh: "Now the body is not for fornication, but for the Lord; and the Lord for the body. And God hath both raised up the Lord, and will also raise up us by His own power. Know ye not that your bodies are the members of Christ? Shall I then take the members of Christ, and make them the members of an harlot?"[12] St Paul went on to equate sex with whoredom, and called for abstinence as much as possible.

St Cyprian of Carthage, whose teachings shaped the day-to-day life of the medieval church and mosque, wrote in the third century, with considerable gusto, against "the peril of human love" and the "lusts of the flesh". One of the precepts which had no small influence on the story of the European whore was his teaching that if a woman invited the eyes of men, called forth their sighs and offered them matter for their lust and fuel for the flames of passion, she must be held guilty of their ruin. Hence a virtuous woman should not venture out of doors adorned and beautified.[13] The repeated advice to married women not to look seductive to their own husbands, and to females in general to avoid being a source of or an object for temptation, is psycho-neurotic if not pathological.

Even marriage was looked upon with disfavour, and many pious people left their marriages unconsummated. Second marriages were only one degree above adultery. The married spouses were barred from the church for a month after a first marriage, for a year after a second marriage and for seven years after a third. The campaign of

The Prostitute in Progressive Literature

ly Fathers coincided with the disintegration of the Roman
d the feeling of impending doom. The extreme strictures of St Jerome caused enough trouble in his own day, and reflected the political anxiety of his world.

Free from the afflictions which accompanied the history of Judeo-Christianity, Islam was able to maintain a great deal of the old joy in sex and earthly pleasures. Yet, under the impact of the former monotheistic faiths, the Muslims soon carried the scourging standard deep into Central Asia and banished whores, temples and all. The wicked seductiveness of women became a main theme in Islamic literature, much as it did in the fiction and drama of Europe.

The reduced position of the harlot slipped lower in the fourteenth and fifteenth centuries, when gonorrhoea and syphilis appeared in the world of brotheldom. The virulence and infectiousness of the disease and the assumption that it had followed promiscuity gave rise to abhorrence of both disease and its victims – for instance the town councils of Aberdeen and Edinburgh tried to control it by branding and segregating the infected.[14] The position of the prostitute naturally suffered as a result and the picture of her wickedness was completed.

A spirit of satanic power was now presumed to exist in the genitalia of all whores. They were burnt, hanged, scourged, whipped and even had their noses cut off. Louis IX issued an edict in 1254 exiling all whores and bawds from France. One Italian commentator, Pietro Aretino, summed up the prevailing views thus: "if a whore ever feels inclined to a man, it is because of a certain craving like that of a pregnant woman, who eats raw garlic and green prunes – and I swear to you ... that lust is the least longing harlots have, for they are always busy thinking how best to tear the heart and liver out of others."[15] The picture of the whore breathing venom during her life and ending tragically at her death became a generally accepted notion which found its expression in various samples of European art and literature. Hogarth painted his famous six pictures of the "Harlot's Progress" in the eighteenth century, depicting the tragic death of the disease-ridden harlot whilst her doctors were arguing about her illness.

Most of the nineteenth-century sociologists, like Iwan Bloch in Germany, painted similar ugly pictures of the whore as a woman whose beauty and femininity were destroyed, whose body was deformed, and whose hair had fallen out. Having replaced her feminine traits with those of males, bold and rough-voiced, she was sought by men only to appease their masochistic desires. Such erroneous notions[16] made their impact on many writers. Whatever sympathies they may have had, they fell under the influence of the Judeo-Christian tradition which allowed the harlot, even the repentant harlot, a soul but not a heart. Thus it was very rare for a novelist or dramatist to let a fallen woman rejoin the respectable folk and lead a normal life. Like the bad boy of Hollywood films, she was not allowed to get away with it. Perhaps we may quote here the memorable description of a harlot's end given by Emile Zola in *Nana*:

> Nana was left alone with upturned face in the light cast by the candle. She was fruit of the charnel-house, a heap of matter and blood, a shovelful of corrupted flesh thrown down on the pillow. The pustules had invaded the whole of her face, so that each touched its neighbour. Fading and sunken, they had assumed the greyish hue of mud, and on that formless pulp, where the features had ceased to be traceable, they already resembled some decaying damp from the grave. One eye, the left eye, had completely foundered among bubbling purulence, and the other, which remained half open, looked like a deep black ruinous hole. The nose was still suppurating. Quite a reddish crust was peeling from one of the cheeks and invading the mouth, which it distorted into a horrible grin. And over this loathsome and grotesque mask of death, the hair, the beautiful hair still blazed like sunlight and flowed downwards in rippling gold. Venus was rotting.

Zola also echoed the old phobic opinion of the whore: "The rage for debasing things was inborn in her. It did not suffice her to destroy them, she must soil them too. Her delicate hands left abominable traces and themselves decomposed whatever they had broken." Indeed, the omnipotent destructive whore is a forerunner of the *femme fatale* who appeared over and over again in French literature.

The Italian writer quoted above wrote his words as a comment on the licentious life of the Republic of Venice during its golden age of commercial prosperity. The affluence of the merchants made the city the centre of European prostitution, where the harlot reached a position as important as that of the Athenian *hetaera*. We are once more facing here the twins of trade and prostitution. The businessman needs the prostitute because of his philistine loveless life, his marriage to money, and his attitude towards all matters in terms of exchange and transaction. Yet the whore is his ruin. One of the moral points aired in Galsworthy's *Forsyte Saga* is that immorality undermines the basis of profit-making. Here we may quote Engels in a different context: "When the producers no longer directly consumed their product, but let it go out of their hands in the course of exchange, they lost control over it. They no longer knew what became of it, and the possibility arose that the product might some day be turned against the producers, used as a means of exploiting and oppressing them."[17] The merchant, having seduced a girl, often his domestic maid, turned her out into the streets as a commodity for circulation, but all the time threatening and eroding the foundations of his establishment – or, as Fauchery, the press reporter in the novel, put it, commenting on Zola's Nana: "With her, the rottenness that was allowed to ferment among the people was rising back up to the aristocracy. She is becoming the force of nature, a power of destruction ... corrupting Paris between her snow-white thighs."

The single-minded profit-making of the merchant and the capitalist required the suppression of all genuine human passions, as was the case with the Puritans. The suppression of sex, that demonic torrent of instinctive feeling, proved to be a harder nut to crack, and the alienated capitalist had to give occasional vent to this impulse in brothels, with orgies of perversion and freedom. Most of the other suppressed human feelings then took advantage of the liberated mood and caught the man off his guard. This is the time for the occasional generosity, joviality and carefree disposition of many otherwise notorious misers and ruthless exploiters. Many wives are often puzzled by the stories of utter carelessness and generosity shown by their skinflint husbands in their nights of revelry. The dreary money-making life of the unlovable banker and its need for costly sexual therapy is reflected in some of the major works of nineteenth-century literature, notably in Balzac and Zola, as will be discussed later.

As the morning comes and the magic of the yellow gold replaces that of the white flesh, the superego takes over and begins its work of torment. True to form, the capitalist resolves the crisis easily by projecting his guilt on to the others, on the whore who made him forget himself and his gold. This conflict of a split personality was theatrically represented by Bertolt Brecht in *Puntila and his Servant, Matti*. In this comedy, Puntila is a rich landowner who, when drunk, becomes very human and generous and offers his own daughter to his driver, Matti; but when he is sober he reverts to his beastly manners and selfish behaviour.

In the process of projection, the capitalist did not sieve his suppressed feelings, but lumped all his sense of guilt and inhumanity together and threw it at the exterior objects which included the prostitute. She became the target of his attack and the symbol of his dark, ugly self. It is no wonder that we find the spokesman of the early English Puritans, Philip Stubbs, recommending death as a penalty for prostitution. This was the darkest period in the history of this profession.

The antithesis of this ideological position is found in the widespread venality and incontinence of society high and low. Giovanni Boccaccio wrote of fourteenth-century Italian society: "From the greatest to the most insignificant, bishops, prelates and temporal lords worshipped voluptuousness in the most disgraceful manner, and abandoned themselves not only to natural but also to unnatural lust without shame or restraint ...."

F. Henriques, the distinguished authority on the history of prostitution, mentions that even nuns competed with the prostitutes for customers. Kings, bishops and emperors built their own brothels to bring in income. The brothels of Southwark, for example, were controlled by the Bishop of Winchester and displayed such names on their signboards as "The Cardinal Hat"![18] Some royal brothels were opened and provided with medical supervision; others were attached to the universities; platoons of whores marched with the armies.[19] Many parish councils in England sold destitute women to professional pimps to avoid maintaining them at the expense of the ratepayers. The parish of Swadlincote ordered the sale of a woman for a florin after her husband had run off.[20]

There was nothing exceptionally cruel about this, for many poor men were known to have sold their own wives to the brothel-keepers. In those days, women had only one of three careers open to them outside domestic slavery: nunnery, sorcery or harlotry. In the Middle Ages, some townspeople pressed the authorities to build special ghettos for the town's harlots. Many town councils responded positively, and the remnants of these brothel quarters may still be seen in many towns and cities. In Russia, prostitutes were forced to carry the yellow cards mentioned by Dostoevsky, and to live in special barracks from which they were not allowed to leave. Only when seriously ill were they permitted, in Warsaw for example, to go out, after a certificate signed by two doctors had been submitted. In Minsk, the regulations allowed them to leave only "in case of death".

The duality of attitude found expression in numerous contradictory passages in the teachings of the ecclesiastical authorities.[21] Augustine described the prostitute as the sewer in a palace; take away the sewer and you fill the palace with pollution; take away prostitution and you fill the world with sodomy. Christ's acceptance of Mary Magdalene was the greatest conciliatory gesture ever made to prostitutes until the rise of socialism. The story continued to arouse the imagination of many priests, prostitutes and thinkers. Many whores, tired of their lives and weary of the psychological struggle, joined the convents. Some of them were obsessed with their redemptive fervour and became saints (St Mary of Egypt, St Pelagia, St Theodatea and St Afra). The redemption of the whore and her conversion to saintliness was the theme treated not only by the Christian idealists of the nineteenth century but also by many revolutionaries and marxists.

The ancient acceptance of prostitution was completely forgotten by the time the new mercantile and capitalist classes emerged as masters of the world within the ideological framework of the Christian church. Their ethos and heritage were based on strict condemnation of fornication and desperate need for it at the same time. The social and radical writers and artists of the modern era were born in this climate of duality and sought, like the writer of the *Gilgamesh* epic, to look at the world around them as reflected in the mirror of the prostitute. The tribes and nations of the Third World, and their thoughts or feelings, did not matter in this context, for this was the world of imperialism. Soon their lands were taken over by its soldiers and their old societies destroyed. With the modern armies of Europe and the United States a new form of prostitution laden with disease and thick with vulgarity, inhumanity, degradation and perversion is introduced. It is the new whoredom of the mass production line. This is the world in which the social and revolutionary writers and artists of the colonial world and the dependent nations were born.

2
Under the Shadow of Capitalism

In reply to Bertrand Russell and the school of free thinkers who referred to the healthy position of respectable prostitution in the ancient world and the East as evidence supporting the call for organized prostitution, the Church of England dismissed the argument as inadmissible because present-day prostitution was based on commercial terms.[1] With the merchants as the first patrons of the prostitute, it is not surprising to see the traffic in female flesh reaching its highest peak under the shadow of the greatest commercial era in history, our own industrial period. The more alienated he became from his human soul by the magic of gold, the greater was the need of contemporary man for sordid diversions.

We first encounter this full-blooded scion of the bourgeoisie in Balzac's *Splendeurs et Misères des Courtisanes* (translated by James Waring as *A Harlot's Progress*). Baron de Nucingen, the Jewish banker with "too many bank notes in his veins" and "a robber on a grand scale, grown fat on the fortunes of the widow and the orphan", becomes hopelessly infatuated with the prostitute Esther, herself (ironically) the daughter of a Jewish prostitute. Like many of the fatal harlots in French literature, Esther is portrayed as ignorant and illiterate. Yet her power over the representatives of the middle class is devastating:

> She bears about her a sort of magic wand by which she lets loose the brutal appetites so vehemently suppressed in men who still have a heart while occupied with politics or science, literature or art. There is not in Paris another woman who can say to the beast as she does, "Come out!" And the beast leaves his lair and wallows in excess. She feeds you up to the chin, she helps you to drink and smoke. In short, this woman is the salt of which Rabelais writes, which, thrown on matter, animates it and elevates it to the marvellous realms of art.

The baron has no family life worthy of note, and the only thing we learn about it is when his wife shows her good understanding of her society and volunteers advice to her doting husband on how to win the whore. The only two worlds in which he feels at home are the Bourse and Esther's house of love; and between the two, the banker hurries backward and forward. In a poignant little scene evoking the romantic scenes of the days of chivalry, the modern knight of the bourgeoisie, fat, ugly, ill-spoken and ignorant, frantically passes under the window of his common whore en route to the Bourse. As Esther appears at the window, according to his instructions, to give him courage, he murmurs heroically: "She is *ein anchel*," pronounced with that "horrible Polish Jewish accent, a jargon which must be as unpleasant to read as it is to hear".

De Nucingen's angel costs him a great deal and consumes all the fortunes of the widow and the orphan in one payment after the other. She is not the old medieval harlot freelancing for herself, but the tool of another ménage of bourgeois robbers. Her over-ambitious gigolo and her scheming protector of a priest demand more and more money from her to finance their diplomatic careers and corrupt church manipulation. To groom her for the task, the false priest, always a target for Balzac, starts by instructing her on Christianity and the proper manners of civilized society. Once baptized and schooled, she is delivered to the sex-starved banker.

Marriage has always been a convenient social structure, but this functionalism reached an extreme of crudity with the advent of capitalism, and the attention of the social writers was immediately drawn to the unnatural state of the bourgeois marriage and its financial opportunism.

Hegel elaborated the concept of "alienation" (*Entfremdung*), which implied the destruction of personal relationships and harmony between individuals in love because of "acquisition and possession of property". He explained that the lover who must look upon his or her beloved as the owner of property must also come to feel his or her particularity, which consists in his being bound up with "dead things", militating against the community of their life.[2]

Bourgeois marriage looked to many thinkers no more than a legalized form of prostitution in which women hired themselves in cold blood to the mechanical gratification of men in return for their upkeep and security with the subsequent result that both parties found their real satisfaction in fornication. The alienated married life of contemporary high society with its variations of domestic misalliances, contracted for financial considerations, became the centrepiece time and time again in modern literature, whether in the Western world or in Afro-Asia.

In *Nicholas Nickleby*, the businessman-moneylender Ralph

Nickleby even weighs marriage in terms of fiscal gain. He himself enters a marriage of convenience, from which his wife manages to run away with the first lover she meets, leaving behind the sickly result of the loveless union, little Smike, the retarded son whom the sadistic father unwittingly tormented and persecuted. To top it all, Mr Nickleby stoops to the vile attempt at procuring his niece, Kate Nickleby, for the well-to-do aristocrats and rich men of his acquaintance in anticipation of gain.

Dickens deals with this subject again in *Dombey and Son*. The earth was made for Dombey & Son to trade in, and the sun and moon to give them light; rivers and seas were formed to float their ships. Mr Dombey marries his wife in the manner of a commercial deal for the recruitment of a trade partner, and his love for his son is no more than the love for Dombey & Son. Every thing around him is stiff, stone-hard and lifeless. Even when he wants to turn to a listener he turns in one piece as if he had no limbs or joints. When the nurse takes little Paul for a walk, it is like a funeral, and when the doctor warns him of his wife's declining health, Dombey feels sorry for having to lose something from his "household possessions, which was well worth the having and could not be lost without sincere regret".

In his second commercially conceived marriage, Mr Dombey finds the counterpart to his enterprising thrift in the lavishness of his new wife, Edith. In a vain attempt to control her extravagance, he appoints his manager, Mr Carker, to supervise her bills, and the manager's new task leads to a love affair and elopement. The parellelism between promiscuity and capitalist accumulation with the underlying psychological orality, the thirst for devouring and acquisition, is poignantly illustrated by Dickens at this juncture:

> Among sundry minor alterations in Mr Carker's life and habits that began to take place at this time, none was more remarkable than the extraordinary diligence with which he applied himself to business and the closeness with which he investigated every detail that the affairs of the house laid open to him. Always active and penetrating in such matters, his lynx-eyed vigilance now increased twenty-fold. Not only did his weary watch keep pace with every present point that everyday presented to him in some new form, but in the midst of these engrossing occupations he found leisure – that is, he made it – to review the past transactions of the firm, and his share in them, during a long series of years. Frequently when the clerks were all gone, the offices dark and empty, and all similar places of business shut up, Mr Carker, with the whole anatomy of the iron room laid bare

before him, would explore the mysteries of books and papers, with the patient progress of a man who was dissecting the minutest nerves and fibres of his subject.

Everything is a matter of hard cash and there is nothing, according to the protagonist, which is more powerful in life than money. In disgust against this ugly world, Edith Dombey draws the knife and warns her lover not to come any nearer to her: "I am a woman who, from her very childhood, has been shamed and steeled. I have been offered and rejected, put up and appraised, until my very soul has sickened. I have not had an accomplishment or grace that might have been a resource to me, but it has been paraded and vended to enhance my value, as if the common crier had called it through the streets."

The banality and inhumanity of bourgeois married life were attacked even more forcefully in *Pot-Bouille* by Emile Zola, who had a great deal to moan about in his own family life. The novel, which aroused a storm of abuse, gave expression to his depressive bouts and enabled him to vent his anger on the false sanctity of middle-class marriage. Men are depicted here as incorrigible villains who leave their wives and seek the company of worthless whores, in keeping with the masochistic notions of Zola and other writers on the subject. Clarisse Bocquet's luxurious flat at Montmartre, bought for her by her doting respectable magistrate, Duveyrier, becomes a den of vice for her various lovers. When Josserand feels uneasy about discussing his daughter's dowry at this place, Duveyrier reassures him: "Why not? We are more comfortable here than anywhere else."

Clarisse, however, feels affronted by his habitual removing of his medallions whenever he visits her. She decides to quit, to the horror of his wife, who dreads having to endure his company and sexual demands, but the magistrate makes it up with his mistress by promising to wear his decorations of honour even in bed with her. The lower he sinks, the more bourgeois she becomes in her demands and lifestyle. In the midst of dirt and squalor, she insists on having a piano teacher for herself; no one is allowed to visit her without formal invitation; everybody is expected to call her Madame; smoking is not permitted in her presence.

The escape from the domesticated banality and limited horizons of wives to the rich sophistication of the hetaera and the courtesan was reversed by the man of commerce to an escape from the gentility and refinement of the acquired wife to the vulgarity and squalor of the street walker. Like Zola, the Danish novelist J.P. Jakobsen portrayed in his Niel Lyhne the character of contemporary man ever tormented by the desire for degraded women. Masochism and guilt were some of the interpretations advanced for this degeneration and alteration in the sexual behaviour of modern times. A series of horrific pictures along such lines were presented by Frank Wedekind's *Earth Spirit* and *Pandora's Box* in the character of Lulu. Set against the background of revolution, financial collapse and large-scale bankruptcies, the play introduces one high-ranking villain after another, from Prince Escerney, who enjoys being kicked about and ridden like a horse by Lulu, to Dr Goli, who risks the virtue of his wife for the sake of witnessing little girls in tights, and the young man who marries a whore who poisoned his mother and killed his father. Everyone marries for money, and when Lulu brings in her men stealthily, she does so when her lover is busy at the Bourse.

The only human person in this gallery of rogues is the lesbian countess Geschwitz, who contracts cholera for the sake of freeing Lulu from prison and offers to sleep with the homosexual Rodrigo to please her. She reflects in her hour of trial: "they eat, drink and make love. I wonder if anyone's ever been made happy by love. Doesn't their happiness consist of being able to sleep better and forget everything? Lord God, I thank thee for not being like other women." Lulu eventually meets her death in London at the hands of Jack the Ripper, who goes on quietly to wipe off his bloody knife, whistling "Land of Hope and Glory" to himself.

England, the mother of the Industrial Revolution, understandably produced the worst examples of fornication. The eighteenth century witnessed the blasphemous clubs, the rape houses for deflowering kidnapped girls, the tea gardens frequented by professional whores, and the bagnios (those public baths which provided sex with flagellation). The Englishman's obsession with taking the virginity of girls as young as twelve years or even younger gave him the reputation, on the Continent, of a child raper. *Fanny Hill* gives a picture of London's sexual life which is by no means completely fictional. In the nineteenth century, *My Secret Life*, published under a pseudonym, amounted to some 900,000 words of autobiography containing episodes which make some of our present perversions appear as children's games.

There were all the elements which propagated prostitution: great economic inequality between the poor and the rich, inequality between men and women, and inequality in the distribution of the sexes. Industrial life shifted masses of men to one corner and masses of women to another. The continuous conflicts over foreign markets required a large number of sailors and soldiers to leave their womenfolk and congregate somewhere else. Traditional family life was disrupted as its members were made into commodities ready for hire wherever, whenever and however the capital required.

This state of affairs developed under the eyes of the pre-war generation in the story of the black migration from the depressed south to the industrial north of the United States, well reflected in *Blood on the Forge*, written in 1941 by the black American novelist William Attaway. The writer himself followed the track of the mass proletarian movement to the north, where he led a wandering life of deprivation and rootlessness during the depression of the Thirties. In this proletarian novel, the class-conscious William Attaway tells the story of Big Mat, who was squeezed out of the southern states by racial pressure and the promises of the factory floor. As he enrols for employment, he finds that his new employer offers transport facilities for the workmen migrating to the north, but not for their families. He therefore takes his place on the travelling truck with his trombone but not his wife. In the midst of the industrial inferno, he meets the fallen Anna, another victim of the American way of life. The two settle together for a life of sin, of course, just for a while before the deluge.

Whoredom could no longer remain a sport pursued by a handful of revellers in one or two friendly houses of a provincial town. Suddenly the profession began to gain an unprecedented momentum reflected in the statistics of the period. During the eighteenth century the number of whores in Paris was 20,000, and in London 50,000.[3] Just before the First World War, the number of registered prostitutes rose to 40,000 in St Petersburg and 30,000 in Vienna. In the 1930s, there were an estimated 99,800 whores in the United States of America, managed by 25,900 pimps. Dr W. Acton, the nineteenth-century authority on the subject, calculated that the number of adult males for every prostitute was eighty in Edinburgh, sixty in London, fifteen in Paris and fifteen in New York.[4]

Two scientific discoveries made the profession easier to practise on a large scale, namely the vulcanization of rubber and safer abortion of women. Just as the discovery of blood transfusion enabled the bourgeoisie to send the casualties back to the field of war, so abortion and contraception enabled it to keep armies of female warriors in brothel-land, a factor which has had a tremendous effect on the story of mass prostitution. Whoredom was recognized as a going concern, and the capitalization of the business was soon introduced. What distinguishes modern prostitution from anything that went before the Industrial Revolution is not its volume but its highly capitalized and sometimes monopolistic character. "Syndicalized prostitution", according to Ben L. Reitman, is the new category of harlotry introduced since the mid-nineteenth century.[5]

S. O'Callaghan spent a few years studying this phenomenon in recent times and found prostitution nearly as internationalized and monopolized as petroleum. The main international syndicate, after the Second World War, was centred in Beirut, with branches operating in Western Europe and Africa. One of the most successful organizations in America, he found, was the Independent Benevolent Association operating among Jewish girls.[6]

During the nineteenth century, the chain brothels owned by the same organization had been already well advanced. One procuress owned twenty-six brothels, and the celebrated Mary Wilson had houses in London's Bond Street, St Pancras and St John's Wood. Another notable procuress, Mrs Berkely, invested £10,000 in an eight-year programme. Henriques goes on to mention that another reputable woman, Mrs Jeffries, discovered the growing appetite for perversion and wanted to cash in on the booming market. She secured capital from a number of wealthy gentlemen and hastened to open a variety of businesses in London, including a brothel exclusively for flagellation in Rose Cottage, and another for assorted perversions off Gray's Inn Road.[7]

As we enter the imperialist stage of capitalism characterized by the export of capital, the international manipulation of prostitution begins to emerge in what is known as "traffic in women" or, sometimes, "white slavery". The *Pall Mall Gazette* was one of the first journals to point to the inter-continental traffic. One procurer said: "I can only speak for Belgium and the north of France. I know nothing of the supply to Bordeaux, Paris, Holland and the rest of the continent. But I should think that, on the average, to these places which I have named, twenty English girls are in the habit of going every month." Another brothel-keeper affirmed that, at two days' notice and for a £10 commission, he could deliver to any place two young girls with a doctor's certificate that each was *virgo intacta*. There were retailers, wholesalers, accredited agents, employment agents, managers and financiers. "The system of procuration", the report sums up, "is reduced to science."[8]

The development called for a counter-effort on an international level, and a series of world conferences were convened from the beginning of this century. The subject was later entrusted to the League of Nations, which set up special commissions that went on studying and reporting through the Twenties and Thirties. The

1927 report remarked that the women were known to alternate and follow each other in a series of centres with a "remarkable regularity" that indicated the existence of an organization moving the whores according to an established plan.[9] The Middle East and Latin America were specially marked as two valuable markets. In 1924, the number of registered imported whores in Cairo was 941, in Port Said 129 and in Alexandria 1,356. In Argentina, there were 1,200 registered prostitutes and between 5,000 and 10,000 unregistered prostitutes.

The League of Nations report on the Far East put Saigon as a centre for operation and China as the main source of supply from which girls were bought for a trifle to swell the number of officially known Chinese whores to 4,000 in Hong Kong, 6,000 in Malaya and 10,000 in Siam. Iraq remained a source of supply to India, whereas the quality prostitutes came from Europe and the United States. Such were the women who could fetch, when sold, as in one instance, as much as $8,000; but native girls were purchased sometimes for no more than £7, which was the price paid by a Beirut procuress to another in Tripoli. Some prostitutes were even pawned at certain banking brothels whilst other cheap places, like Hong Kong and Macao, were used as depots for regrouping and redistribution. Once more the report speaks of "places of the Middle East and the Far East to which traffic is facilitated by the existence of brothels from a network within the bounds of which women are moved from one centre of exploitation to another".[10]

This is the vital difference which separated the bourgeois idealists from the radical socialists in their treatment of the prostitution theme. Whether it is Zola's Nana, Tolstoy's Maslova, Dostoevsky's Sonya or Maupassant's Boule de Suif, the prostitute was a woman who slipped into vice for one reason or another, followed her lonely career by herself and met her end of destruction or salvation as an individual. In this, they were like those who look at the pawnbroker round the corner as the real exploiter of society. The socialist writers, on the other hand, saw behind the casual individual the frightening apparatus which was manipulating her and the thousands of individuals like her in the service of the world of capital. Bernard Shaw and Bertolt Brecht were the two socialist dramatists who grasped this character of capitalist prostitution. They were supported in this by the social democratic thinker August Bebel, who paid particular attention to the question of prostitution and reached the conclusion in his *Women and Socialism* that this profession had become an institution as organized and established as any other institution of bourgeois society.

Bernard Shaw had no direct knowledge of the underworld life of London's brothels, a disadvantage which he was able to turn to credit by looking not at the prostitute herself but at the question of prostitution. From his intellectual summits he could see the masses of victims and parasites swarming in the swamps of capitalist society. He had cast this glance in the direction of brotheldom at the call of his friend Beatrice Webb, who happened to read Guy de Maupassant's short story "Yvette" and was inspired to ask Shaw to create a modern version of the heroine of that name.

Maupassant's Yvette, the daughter of a fallen woman, is baffled by the determination of Jean de Servigny not to marry her, although they are both in love. She keeps wondering what is wrong with her until she discovers the truth about her mother. The daughter now turns to her mother and asks her to leave this life of "gilded prostitution", whereby she gives Maupassant his cue. The mother puts the case of the economic plight of the poor which drives them to any vice: "When you are only a poor servant girl with fifty francs of savings, you must get away from it somehow if you don't want to rot in the workhouse; and there's only one way for women, only one way, do you hear, when you are a servant! We can't make fortunes on the stock exchange or at high finance. We've nothing but our bodies." She turns to the girl who owes her refinement to her mother's immoral earnings, and lashes out at the hypocrisy of the middle class: "And your honest women, do they go without? It's they who are sluts, because they're not forced. They've money to live on and amuse themselves with; they have their lovers out of wantonness. It's they who are sluts." With pride and defiance she exclaims: "I am as good as any other woman, do you hear? I am a harlot, it's true, and I am proud of it; I am worth a dozen of your honest women."

Yvette is stabbed with the realities of her society and decides to kill herself with chloroform. The effect of the chemical numbs her feelings and reveals to her the beauty of the world. She stops short of death and comes back to life in the arms of her beloved. Servigny promises to love her and goes out singing:

"*Souvent femme varie*
Bien fol est qui s'y fie."

Beatrice Webb, as an ardent advocate of women's emancipation and a socialist, could not accept the realistic ending of Maupassant or the feminine weakness of his heroine. In a letter to the *Daily Chronicle* (30 July 1898) Shaw wrote:

Miss Janet Achurch mentioned to me a novel by some French

writer as having a dramatic story in it. She told me the story, which was ultra-romantic. I said, "I will work out the truth about the matter one day." The following autumn, a lady [Beatrice Webb] suggested to me that I should put on the stage a really modern young lady of the governing class – not the sort of thing that theatrical and critical authorities imagine such a lady to be.

G.B.S. did work out the truth one day, and the result was *Mrs Warren's Profession*.

Unlike the romantic Yvette, Shaw's heroine Vivie is a graduate in mathematics and science, looking forward to a successful career in the city. One thing, however, detracts from her accomplishments. Everything is owed to the immoral earnings of her mother, Mrs Warren. On the revelation of this fact, Vivie is revolted, but the mother tells her the full story – how she was one of four illegitimate girls, one of whom died of poisoning in a white lead factory, how the second had to maintain three children and a drunken husband, and the other two sisters saved themselves by taking up prostitution and becoming respectable women of high society, running well-kept brothels where no girl died of lead poisoning. "Do you think we were such fools as to let other people trade in on our good looks by employing us as shopgirls, or barmaids, or waitresses, when we could trade in them ourselves and get all the profits instead of starvation wages?"

The businesslike Vivie sees the point but wonders whether her mother would not really advise her daughter to marry a labourer or work in a factory rather than be a prostitute. "Of course not," replied Mrs Warren. "What sort of mother do you take me for! How could you keep your self-respect in such starvation and slavery?" For the sake of her own and her daughter's respect, Mrs Warren took up prostitution. Vivie is filled with admiration: "My dear mother: you are a wonderful woman: you are stronger than all England." Vivie's admiration, however, turns sour. Now that they have both arrived and made a substantial enough fortune, she expects her mother to give up. Mrs Warren may be stronger than all England but both she and all England are slaves to capital. She is only a managing director on behalf of a vast syndicate of brothels extending to Ostend, Brussels, Vienna and Budapest. The Reverend Gardner and Sir George Croft are all in it. At 35 per cent per annum, Sir George is pleased to have a stake of £40,000 in the business:

> Why the devil shouldn't I invest my money that way? I take the interest on my capital like other people: I hope you don't think I

dirty my own hands with the work. Come! You wouldn't refuse the acquaintance of my mother's cousin the Duke of Belgravia because some of the rents he gets are earned in queer ways. You wouldn't cut the Archbishop of Canterbury, I suppose, because the Ecclesiastical Commissioners have a few publicans and sinners among their tenants. So you remember your Crofts scholarship at Newham? Well, that was founded by my brother the MP. He gets his 22 per cent out of a factory with 600 girls in it, and not one of them getting wages enough to live on. How d'ye suppose they manage when they have no family to fall back on? Ask your mother. And do you expect me to turn my back on 35 per cent when all the rest are pocketing what they can, like sensible men? No such fool! If you're going to pick and choose your acquaintances on moral principles, you'd better clear out of this country, unless you want to cut yourself out of all decent society.

Vivie answers him unrelentingly: "When I think of the society that tolerates you, and the laws that protect you! When I think how helpless nine out of ten young girls would be in the hands of you and my mother! The unmentionable woman and her capitalist bully .... " Armed with the knowledge and will of the modern woman, she leaves mother, lover and all behind to start on her career of actuarial calculations at Lincoln's Inn. The encounter between the mother and her daughter became a source of inspiration for the pioneers of women's liberation movements in many countries including the People's Republic of China, where *Mrs Warren's Profession* became one of the few Western plays which occupied an important place in their repertoire.

Mrs Warren's Profession came soon after *Widowers' Houses*, in which Harry Trench discovers the corrupt source of his fiancée's income, the exploitation of poor tenants. But unlike Vivie, he and his fiancée succumb to the allurement of immoral wealth. G.B.S. was able to argue for and against the methods of Mrs Warren and Mr Sartorius without much difficulty or care because to him what mattered was the system. During the controversy over the morality of the play, he wrote:

> Nothing would please our sanctimonious British public more than to throw the whole guilt of Mrs Warren's profession on Mrs Warren herself. Now the whole aim of my play is to throw that guilt on the British public .... The notion that prostitution is created by the wickedness of Mrs Warren is as silly as the notion that drunkenness is created by the wickedness of the publican.

Shaw's ending of his plays had always left his audiences

disorientated, but the ending of *Mrs Warren's Profession* was considered by many critics as a disappointing anticlimax. Frank Harris, Shaw's friend and biographer, said that Shaw had never written a play "as full of magnificent misses" as this one. Just when he came to finish off the conventional values of his society, he pulled his punches at the last moment.[11] Having established the strong moral position of the prostitute in the midst of the capitalist jungle, he demolished it by turning the rationalist Vivie against it.

Outside his intellectual crusade, Shaw had in fact lived a Victorian life with its values of respectability and decency. One of the accepted notions of that life was that a prostitute should never be allowed to get away with it, a standpoint which shaped the plot, characters and ending of most stories dealing with the life of a whore. Shaw himself looked back at the play with horror – "this awful piece of mine". To Janet Achurch, he described Mrs Warren as "a most deplorable old rip".[12] Yet, on further consideration of the play, it appears that Vivie's revolt had only flared up on her discovery of the dimension and continuation of the business. She admired her mother when she was a poor woman trying to give herself and her child a more dignified life by putting her body to a better use. She hated her mother when she became the head of a syndicate amassing wealth at the expense of poorer girls. From a hired labourer, her mother had become an exploiter of labour on an international scale. The play, of course, suffered artistically from this undramatic transformation in its leading character. "In *Mrs Warren's Profession*", Shaw wrote to R. Golding Bright, "you had the procuress, the organizer of prostitution, convicting society of her occupation. All three plays [*Mrs Warren's Profession, The Philanderer* and *Widowers' Houses*] were criticism of a special phase, the capitalist phase, of modern social organization ...."[13]

Whatever reading one might give to the play, the rejection of the whore did not save the author from the censor. The play, as Frank Harris remarked at the time, "was not up to sufficient standard of immorality". Vivie's ambiguous parenthood allowed the possibility of her being the sister of her lover and the daughter of the parson with the fiery youth and the sermons bought from others, as described in the play. This was considered a piece of indecency, and the play was banned, only to open the widest field for G.B.S. to enjoy himself in one of the longest fights of his life. "We are allowed and encouraged", he said, "to make the stage an attractive advertisement for prostitution and to drive the young to the brothel by the most potent of aphrodisiacs; but when I dramatized the truth about prostitution in *Mrs Warren's Profession*, the play was at once prohibited."[14] G.B.S. challenged the Lord Chamberlain to mention any extremity of secual misconduct presentable on the stage which had not been presented under his licence. He further offered to submit his play to any panel of judges who did not include people who profiteered from prostitution, used it or found its value indispensable as a safety valve protecting their family life.

Sir John Ervine, a contemporary biographer, compared Shaw's incest implication with T.S. Eliot's more definite case of incest in *A Confidential Clerk*, and pointed out that it was due to Shaw's efforts that Eliot was able to stage his play.[15] The incest side was by no means the real cause of the trouble, which was the indictment of the very foundation of society, something which T.S. Eliot had never attempted. The fate of *Mrs Warren's Profession* was even more frustrating in the United States, where the entire company were arrested, the manager prosecuted, the theatre closed and the play hunted from town to town, adding one financial disaster to another to both manager and playwright. Shaw's cardinal guilt was that he sent to America *Mrs Warren's Profession* and not Mrs Warren herself. Had he done the latter, his bank account would have shown a remarkably different balance. The Police Commissioner's report was typical: "There are six characters. The leading ones profess to have led or are leading immoral lives. They continue to be prosperously immoral to the end of the play which to my mind was revolting, indecent, nauseating, where it was not boring." For allowing a prostitute to enjoy even the fruit of her downfall, the play was described by American critics as a pigsty, illuminated gangrene, a suppuration of a plague spot, to quote only a few.

The fact that Bernard Shaw and other socialist writers had recognized in the prostitute the emblem of bourgeois society is very clear, but what is more interesting is the manner in which the members of that society themselves were able to recognize in the harlot their own image, which they projected on her. The reflection was terrifying and to allow that image to go unpunished, as Shaw had done, would not serve the psychological mechanism of projection, i.e. to punish in her what they should otherwise have punished in themselves. Shaw had only presented the capitalization of prostitution to arouse the American Police Commission. He was careful enough not to complete the picture of modern prostitution by bringing in the other component, the authority represented by its corrupt police. This challenge was left to a more formidable revolutionary obsessed with capitalist prostitution – Bertolt Brecht.

The German poet, however, was preceded in this by the Austrian Frank Wedekind, who joined a group of revolutionary intellectuals in forming the Simplicissimus movement, which dedicated its literary activities to denouncing the evils of German imperialism. Wedekind's whore Lulu (the plays were written between 1892 and 1894) falls in her various adventures into the tentacles of an international vice syndicate engaged in exporting European prostitutes to the flourishing brothel-land of Cairo. The German-born whore refuses the attempt and kills the homosexual Rodrigo in fear of him denouncing her to the police. The detective Casti-Piani starts to exploit his position in intimidating Lulu into joining the Cairo market, and finally brings the police force to arrest her, only to find that she has anticipated his move by fleeing to Britain to resume her career freely there. In utter disappointment, the police officer murmurs at this discovery: "There is something wrong with the system."

3
Victims of Circumstance

Most of the prostitutes mentioned in this study were set by their creators against a background of poverty and need. In *Nana*, Emile Zola introduces a series of common whores hailing from such a social environment; Lucy Steward is the daughter of a railwayman; Caroline Hequet is an orphan with a dissipated mother; Blanche de Sevry comes from a poor village near Amiens; Clarisse Besnus was brought to Paris as a domestic servant; Simonne Cabiroche is the daughter of a furniture dealer; Tatan Néné herded cows in the country. John Galsworthy's Chloe, Balzac's Esther, Dickens's Nancy, Wedekind's Lulu, Dostoevsky's Sonya and Nastasya all come from depressed conditions.

One of the earliest novels dealing with this relationship between poverty and prostitution was Mary Wollstonecraft's *Maria, or the Wrongs of Women*, written in the eighteenth century to deal with the individual stories of hapless domestic maids seduced and exploited by their masters and eventually kicked out of their situations, pregnant and penniless. Again, the doomed fate of the prostitute is projected here in Jemima's vain attempt to escape from the life of vice and find respectable employment.

One of the rare statistical surveys conducted in tsarist Russia among the brothel population in 1889 revealed that 83.5 per cent of prostitutes had suffered extreme poverty and 65 per cent of them had been in domestic service. It did not take long for the sociologists and social thinkers of the nineteenth century to take note of the bleak position of women, accentuated by the Industrial Revolution, and the resultant life of prostitution and delinquency. Behind all the obsession of Charles Dickens with the fate and career of the prostitute lies his early sociological research into the economic conditions of women, their exploitation and their exposure to prostitution, which was evidenced in his early sketch "Shops and their Tenants".

Both Parent-Duchatelet, the French authority on prostitution, and Henry Mayhew in England emphasized the connection between the social evil and poverty, and most observers reflected that brothel life was far more satisfactory than the blessings of an industrial family life, or as Dr Acton put it at the time:

> If we compare the prostitute at thirty-five with her sister, who perhaps is the married mother of a family, or has been a toiling slave for years in the over-heated laboratories of fashion, we shall seldom find that the constitutional ravages often thought to be necessary consequences of prostitution exceed those attributable to the cares of a family and the heart-wearing struggles of virtuous labour.[1]

Mayhew also focused on the adverse conditions encountered by London's prostitutes, and quoted from his interviews with them. One girl, who was only sixteen when she ran away from her cruel and violent mistress and joined the life of vice, described her lonely living in a lodging house in London:

> I have known between three and four dozen boys and girls sleep in one room. The beds were horridly filthy and full of vermin. There were very wicked carryings on. The boys, if any difference was the worst. We lay packed on a full night, a dozen boys and girls squeezed into one bed. That was very often the case – some at the foot and some at the top – boys and girls all mixed. I can't go into all the particulars, but whatever could take place in words or acts between boys and girls did take place and in the midst of the others ... some boys and girls slept without any clothes, and would dance about the room that way.[2]

Like Acton, Mayhew agreed that the general state of prostitutes was better than that of the virtuous wives of similar social standing. The temptation to break away from the degradation of honest living manifested itself therefore to any intelligent, deprived woman. In this we have the testimony of the real Dame aux Camélias (Marie Duplessis, the Parisian courtesan who came from a poverty-stricken home in a Normandy village) in one of her numerous letters: "Why did I sin myself? Because honest work would never have earned me the luxury for which I craved irresistibly. Whatever I may seem to you, I swear I am not covetous or debauched. I wanted to know the pleasures and refinements of artistic taste, the joy of living in elegant and cultivated society." But she had to pay dearly for these pleasures, dying of consumption, poor and abandoned, at the age of twenty-three.

"It is so often asked: Why does she choose it?" reflected a more articulate Frenchwoman, Simone de Beauvoir. "The question is rather, why has she not chosen it?"³ The pressure of economic need brought about by the capitalist convulsion was amply recorded in modern social literature. In *Skin Game* (1920) John Galsworthy puts on stage the character of the hapless Chloe Hornblower, driven to a compromised life under the control of vice agents as a result of her father's bankruptcy and destitution. Life smiles on her for a while when she meets and marries the prosperous Hornblower, son of a parvenu industrialist, but the conflict which arises between this family of upstarts and the old-established, less prosperous Hillcrests brings back the ghost of her former life and sets in motion her tragic end. In vain does she try to justify her past to the more fortunate – "You have never been right down in the mud."

A different set of events and circumstances were plotted by Thomas Hardy for another victim of contemporary society in *Tess of the D'Urbervilles* (1891), the story of a poor girl whose family came from a once prosperous and aristocratic house. The plight of her needy father prompts her to seek the help of the wealthy Elec D'Urbevilles, a man with a doubtful claim to that artistic name, but representing the influence and riches of the new British middle class. The attempt leads to the seduction and pregnancy of Tess, and she goes back to her parents to deliver the fruit of her weakness. The author dwells on the subject of sin and retribution:

> One may indeed admit the possibility of a retribution lurking in the present catastrophe. Doubtless some of Tess Durbeyfield's male ancestors rollicking home from a fray dealt the same measure even more ruthlessly towards peasant girls of their time. But though to visit the sins of the fathers on the children may be a morality good enough for divinities, it is scorned by average human nature and does not therefore mend the matter.

Yet Thomas Hardy seems to have accepted the traditional notion of divine retribution, as Tess delivers a sickly child who soon expires despite all her care and attention. A moving scene follows in which she discovers that the little infant has not been baptized and sees visions of demons and fire of hell tormenting him to eternity. Rejected by her father and the village priest, she performs an improvised baptism and leads the funeral by herself:

> So the baby was carried in a small deal box under an ancient woman shawl to the churchyard that night and buried by lantern light at the cost of a shilling and a pint of beer to the sexton in that shabby corner of God's allotment where he lets the nettles grow and where all unbaptized infants, notorious drunkards, suicides and other conjecturally damned are laid.

Under the cover of darkness, Tess steals her way to the little grave to lay a small cross of sticks and puts it there with a few flowers in a jar of water bearing the label "Keelwell's Marmalade".

The sealed fate of the fallen woman in Victorian England unfolds itself in the story of Angel Clare, the liberal and progressive idealist whom Tess meets and falls in love with. Clare leaves the career of priesthood to follow a Tolstoyan life based on tilling the land and living with rural people. Tess presents him with his ideal woman, but the discovery of her past unmasks the hypocrisy of his idealism and contrasts it with the harsh realities. On the day of their marriage he tells her of his past moral lapses, and the innocent woman reciprocates, much against the advice of her earthy mother, by telling him of her past experience. The man of God and ideals turns against her, and in vain does she try to win his forgiveness:

> "Oh, Tess, forgiveness does not apply to the case. You were one person. You are now another ..."
> "Don't, don't, it kills me quite bad. Oh, have mercy on me, have mercy. Angel, what do you mean by that laugh? Do you know what this is to me? I thought, Angel, that you love me, me, my very self. If it is 'I' you do love, how can it be that you look and speak so? It frightens me."
> "I repeat, the woman I have been loving is not you."
> "How?"
> "Another woman in your shape."

Tess is rejected and forced once more to face the choice between sharing the life of destitution with her parents and brothers or accepting a life of sin with her former ravisher. Like most sensible women she accepts the second alternative, but the decision leads to the inevitable tragic end of the fallen woman of nineteenth-century literature. Tess kills her lover and goes to the gallows. Yet this end was not enough to pacify the champions of established morality who took particular exception to the subtitle of the novel, "A Pure Woman". For many years, the author could not publish the entire work without deleting a number of scenes, including the baptism of the illegitimate infant, and the play version could only be staged in 1926, when Hardy was an old man of eighty-six.

In classifying his works, Hardy included *Tess of the D'Urbervilles* in the category of "Novels of Character and Environment", a notion which was in keeping with the general view of fallen women, courtesans and common prostitutes. In most of the nineteenth-century drama and fiction connected with the life and fate of such women, there is an element of acceptance that some women are destined by their nature to fall from grace. Even Dickens was overwhelmed by this phenomenon, and wrote in one of his letters to Miss Scouts:

> There is no doubt that many of them would go on well for some time, and would then be seized with a violent fit of the most extraordinary passion, apparently quite motiveless, and insist on going away. There seems to be something inherent in their course of life which engenders and awakens a sudden restlessness and recklessness; and which may be long suppressed, but breaks out like madness; and which all people who have had opportunities of observation in penitentiaries and elsewhere, must have contemplated with astonishment and pity.[4]

Emile Zola followed a similar line of thought, not as a corollary of personal involvement and clinical observations, like Dickens, but in response to the psychological and eugenic theories of his times, which gave his prostitutes their demonic and fatalist qualities. But as we have noted in the case of Hardy, the reformers and social writers balanced this trend with the element of environment, and their work seemed to serve as a transitional phase before the full commitment of the socialist and marxist school to the economic factor, a matter which calls for a brief survey.

Marx's early writings – mainly between 1844 and 1846 – evolved around the Hegelian concept of alienation, and developed it into an economic analysis of the capitalist society in which the animal becomes human and the human animal; the senses, the primary sources of freedom and happiness, are reduced to one "sense of possessing"; the object of love is looked upon as something which may or may not be able to be appropriated. Even the modes of pleasure and enjoyment change from their free and "universal nature" into modes of "egotistic" possession and acquisition. Human beings become related to each other only through the commodities they produce, and the individual desires and capacities have no part in the evaluation. Capitalist commodity production has the mystifying effect of transforming the social relations between people into a matter of money, under the impact of what Marx calls in *Capital* "the fetishism of commodities, which leads to a complete negation of humanity".[5]

In his essay of 1844, "Human Requirements and Division of Labour Under the Rule of Private Property", Marx relates the concept of alienation to the subject of morality and points out that the significance of the forces of human nature is reversed under private property so as to make every person speculate on creating a new need in the others and on seducing them into a mode of enjoyment and economic ruin. The increase in the quantity of objects is therefore accompanied by an extension of the alien powers to which man is subjected. The extension of products and needs becomes an ever-calculating subservience to "inhuman, sophisticated, unnatural and imaginary appetites". This estrangement produces a bestial barbarism and crude simplicity of needs. Having explained how people have become willing to sacrifice their lives to dead commodities and artificially created needs, Marx goes on to attack the political economists and their morality, which is based on the denial of life and human needs. The less you eat, the less you drink and buy books, the less you go to the theatre, the less you love, sing and paint, the greater becomes your treasure which neither moths nor rust will devour – your capital. "The less you are, the less you express yourself, the more you have, i.e. the greater is your alienated life, the greater is the store of your estranged being."

Everything is determined, according to political economy, the gospel of capitalist morality, by its usefulness. It teaches us that we must not stint the gratification of our senses and must spare ourselves all sharing of general interest, all sympathy, all trust, etc ....

> You must make everything that is yours saleable, i.e. useful. If I ask the political economist: Do I obey economic laws if I extract money by offering my body for sale, by surrendering it to another's lust? (The factory workers in France call prostitution of their wives and daughters the ninth working hour, which is literally correct.) – Or am I not acting in keeping with political economy if I sell my friend to the Moroccans .... Then the political economist replies to me: You do not transgress my laws ....

Prostitution is therefore, according to Marx, the most logical career for the capitalist way of life, and he goes on to conclude that only with the establishment of communism can we expect the disappearance of such unnatural phenomena.[6]

The exploitation of labour found its ugliest form in the exploitation of female workers who were introduced to industry, according to Marx, because they were cheaper than machinery, and he went on to relate in *Capital* the story of Mary Anne Walkly, the milliner who died of work in 1863 after working without intermission for $26\frac{1}{2}$ hours, sustained by sherry, port or coffee.

In his *Condition of the Working Classes in England*, Frederick Engels sets out to make it plain that "the social order makes family life almost impossible", and goes on to describe the kind of life enjoyed by the ordinary working-class family:

> ... the husband works the whole day through, perhaps the wife also and the elder children, all in different places; they meet night and morning only, all under perpetual temptation to drink; what family life is possible under such conditions? Yet the working man cannot escape from the family, must live in the family, and the consequence is a perpetual succession of family troubles, domestic quarrels, most demoralizing for parents and children alike. Neglect of all domestic duties, neglect of the children especially, is only too common among English working people, and only too vigorously fastened by the existing institutions of society. And children growing up in this savage way, amidst the demoralizing influence, are expected to turn out goody-goody and moral in the end. Verily, the requirements are naive, which the self-satisfied bourgeois makes upon the working man.[7]

When people are placed under brutal conditions which appeal to the brute only, what remains to them but to rebel or succumb to utter brutality, he asks. Moreover the bourgeoisie does its full share in maintaining prostitution and swelling the number of prostitutes, who fill the streets of London every evening, to 40,000. "How many of them owe it to the seduction of a bourgeois, that they must offer their bodies to the passers-by in order to live? Surely, it [the bourgeoisie] has least of all a right to reproach the workers with sexual brutality."[8]

Both Marx and Engels make various references to the restricted choice of poor women between starvation and prostitution, but Engels goes further in *The Origin of the Family* to assert that in fact the whole bourgeois form of marriage is no more than prostitution. This is best reflected in the kind of German novel where Protestant monogamy leads merely to "a wedded life of leaden boredom, which is described as domestic bliss" and the young man gets his girl; and in those French novels where typically the husband gets the cuckold's horns.

> In both cases, however, marriage is determined by the class position of the participants, and to that extent always remains marriage of convenience. In both cases, the marriage of convenience often turns into the crassest prostitution – sometimes on both sides, but much more generally on the part of the wife, who differs from the ordinary courtesan only in that she does not hire out her body, like a wage worker, on piecework, but sells it into slavery once for all. Just as in grammar two negatives make a positive, so in the morals of marriage, two prostitutions make one virtue.[9]

The typical form of married life for capitalist society is that of monogamy supplemented by adultery and prostitution; the old traditional hetaerism is changed by capitalist commodity production into an unconcealed form of prostitution with all its demoralizing effects. But: "We are now approaching a social revolution in which the hitherto existing economic foundations of monogamy will disappear just as certainly as will those of its supplement – prostitution." Engels, however, turns the argument in another direction to conclude that with the conversion of the means of production into social property, the necessity for a certain statistically calculable number of women to surrender themselves for money will vanish. "Prostitution disappears; monogamy, instead of declining, finally becomes reality – for the men as well."[10]

These words have become the guidelines for socialist writers to this day, and marxist thinkers have always shown an acceptance of venality as part of the existing capitalist society. It was from this standpoint that Lenin lashed out in 1913 against the fifth international conference in London on white slave traffic, which called for combating prostitution by a combination of religion and police: "From this one can judge what disgusting bourgeois hypocrisy reigns at these aristocratic-bourgeois conferences. The mountebank of charity and the police protectors of mockery at want and misery together to 'fight against prostitution', which is maintained precisely by the aristocrats and the bourgeoisie...."[11] On a later occasion, he sent out another outcry: "Down with this fraud! Down with the liars who are talking of freedom and equality for all, while there is an oppressed sex...."[12]

Once at the head of the Soviet government, and engaged in the great task of state-building, Lenin showed a marked reduction of libido and adopted in some instances positions which were reminiscent of English puritanism. He attacked Sigmund Freud for over-concentration on sexual matters, and criticized German female revolutionaries for devoting their time to discussion of sex and marriage rather than politics and revolution. "I could scarcely believe my ears," he said when he heard that Soviet party workers held similar discussions and studied a pamphlet on sexual problems. "What a waste!" The task of Soviet women was to concentrate on the revolution and socialist reconstruction, and any "poking about in sexual matters" was repulsive; to Soviet youth, he gave a general warning against sexual liberation, which he considered as "an extension of bourgeois brothels". The problems of women and sex would only be solved by the victory of socialism.[13]

In his speech to women workers in 1919,[14] Lenin maintained that not one state in the world had achieved equality between men and women, but Russia had within the very brief period of the revolution liberated women from their degraded position and established complete equality with men. Yet this legal equality, he went on to warn, was not enough and must be consolidated by emancipation from domestic slavery, that is by going out to work. For this purpose, suitable institutions should be set up to help women join their menfolk at the factories and offices. Among such institutions were the reformatories opened for the specific task of reclaiming the prostitute, an undertaking which has become a set-piece for any country taken over by a marxist government. The effort attracted the personal attention of the Soviet leader, who attended the first conference convened by the prostitutes of Russia and addressed them as "Comrades!" This must have been a fine tribute to the tears which the Russian revolutionary was reported to have shed in London after seeing a stage performance of *La Dame aux Camélias*. Lenin was unaware of the evidence that prostitutes over the centuries were inwardly religious and conservative and were rightly represented in literature with a royalist mentality.

Almost all marxist leaders and thinkers come to accept this somewhat Victorian attitude to the future of sex and marriage. The British communist leader William Gallacher repeated Engels's forecast that under socialism, monogamy would be strengthened and married couples would be able to produce more children.[15]

All these ideas had their impact on the radical artists, dramatists and novelists who advocated the socialist solution, and the case of Bernard Shaw may serve as an individual example.

In *The Intelligent Woman's Guide to Socialism and Capitalism*, he repeats the general marxian observation that women suffer more than men from the extremity of the capitalist system and are forced to struggle to entrap men to subsidize their reduced earning – marriage for them becomes compulsory and loveless. Trapped between domestic enslavement and industrial drudgery, women find in prostitution the best solution. "In short capitalism acts on women as a continual bribe to enter into sex relations for money."[16] According to Shaw, prostitution offered women a better chance to preserve their youth than employment in a factory where they might contract necrosis of the jawbone from phosphorus poisoning. As for venereal diseases, there were more women infected with VD by their husbands than by their lovers, and a married woman was as exposed to drugs and alcoholism as a prostitute was. "If a woman accepts capitalist morality, and does what pays her best, she will take what district visitors call (when poor women are concerned) the wages of sin rather than the wages of sweated labour." In reviewing *The*

Conversion of England, a religious play of a sort, Shaw attacked the church as one of the institutions which swelled the number of prostitutes by impoverishing women; it even employed them in the manufacture of sacred books on terms which made the prostitution of a certain percentage of them compulsory.[17]

In his preface to *Getting Married*, Shaw bursts forth with a typical socialist defence of the prostitute in which he alludes to her role as the angel of vengeance:

> We shall continue to maintain the white slave trade and protect its exploiters by, on the one hand, tolerating the white slave as the necessary breakwater of marriage; and on the other, trampling on her and degrading her until she has nothing to hope from our courts, and so, with policemen at every corner, and law triumphant all over Europe, she will still be smuggled and cattle driven from one end of the civilized world to the other, cheated, beaten, bullied, and hunted into the streets to disgusting overwork, without daring to utter the cry for help that brings not rescue but exposure and infamy, yet revenging herself terribly in the end by scattering blindness and sterility, pain and disfigurement, insanity and death among us with the certainty that we are much too pious and genteel to allow such things to be mentioned with a view to saving either her or ourselves from them.[18]

"The necessary breakwater of marriage" is Shaw's metaphor for the capitalist social need for prostitution. The economic conditions of the existing society made it impossible for many people to get married early enough to dispose of the need for premarital sex, and the protection of other people's wives made it prudent to provide a pool of prostitutes. This must be even more imperative because of the nature of the contemporary marriage institution. Capitalism forced not only the bourgeoisie but the proletariat as well to enter into loveless marriages of convenience, which he called in *Man and Superman* "the trade unionism of the married". This form of relationship had nothing to do with the function of sex in improving the human species, the central idea in Shavian thought.

Here again, Shaw endorsed the standard marxian position and accepted the monogamous marriage, free from capitalist constraints and open to simplified divorce, as the future form of social organization. When young women found honourable and comfortable livelihoods on reasonable terms, when young men could afford to get married and when reforms made it easy to dissolve unsuccessful marriages, the streets would make no more recruits and "both prostitution and bachelordom will die a natural death".[19]

This oversimplified equation of poverty with venality reduced a great many socialist literary works in this field to mere economic commentaries, and deprived them of the psychological depth and complexity associated with the life and fate of the prostitute.

4

Brecht and his Underworld

In his comments on *Mrs Warren's Profession*, Bernard Shaw cited her "high English virtues" of vitality, thrift, energy, wise care of her daughter and managing capacity which should make her as good as any other middle-class woman, if not better. Inspired by the marxist assessment of the prostitute as no more than any other person selling her wares and hiring her labour under the accepted rules of capitalist political economy, the socialists rejected the bourgeois treatment of the common whore as a freak phenomenon, too wicked for words or too good to be true, something that was outside the body social. To socialist writers, the prostitute was not just a member of the private property society but the quintessence of that society. This identification of the bourgeoisie with brotheldom was taken to its furthest point by Bertolt Brecht, who pitched his tent in the heart of the underworld when he explored the theme of the capitalist jungle. In his instructions to the actors, he insisted that the parts of the pimps, whores, thieves and cut-throats should never be acted in the conventional uncouth manner expected by the audience. They should be dressed and acted as respectable and refined bourgeois characters no different from the highest figures of society.[1] The brothel itself should look like "a true middle-class idyll". In his notes on *The Threepenny Opera* and its harlots, he gave his stage directions this peculiar marxist context:

> The ladies are in undisturbed possession of their means of production. But for that reason they must not give the impression of being free. For them, democracy does not grant that freedom which it does to all those from whom the means of production can be taken away.[2]

Brecht was a man completely different from Shaw. He learned his craft not under the reign of good Queen Victoria but during the hectic years of the Weimar Republic, and the society he mixed with was not the society of the elegant ladies and gentlemen who wanted to save the *status quo* by putting it on a firmer basis. Brecht's society was made up of rebels, nihilists, revolutionaries, marxists and hippies, to use a more current term. To them, the starting point was the demolition of the *status quo*. Those were the years of a humiliating national defeat, the fall of the German mark, the recession of the late Twenties, mass unemployment, political chaos, corruption in public life and scandalous immoralities among all classes. This was the life depicted by the artists of the expressionist school, the writers of the Neue Sachlichkeit and the virulent brush of Otto Dix and George Grosz.

Brecht was a medical student and worked during the First World War as a medical orderly. The keen eye of the physiologist enabled him to look at people not from an intellectual peak as Shaw had done but from the close range of the microscope. His years were not spent in the British Museum, but in the cafés and beer cellars of Munich and Berlin, teeming with sluts, layabouts, fiery intellectuals and devil-take-all rebels.

Brecht was able to probe deep into the gangrene of the bourgeoisie and see the extent of its decay. It was not only the individual capitalist who had his money involved in the profession; the police, the law and the banks were in it too. *The Threepenny Opera*, his first major exercise in the subject, depicts the three branches of bourgeois decay: robbery, beggary and harlotry. Mr Peachum runs a monopoly of beggary in London, hunting anybody who tries to compete with the syndicate. Macheath runs a counterpart organization for robbery with branches all over England. Both run their organizations with the best business methods and good bookkeeping, with directors and accountants. Among the principal commitments of the chairman is to get the girls (or ladies, as Brecht insists on calling them) pregnant so that they can plead not responsible for their actions. "One needs the physique of a stallion for this job," one gangster remarks when it falls to his lot to deputize for Macheath. Prostitution is thus harnessed in support of both branches; so is the police. Macheath is, in fact, no more than a business partner of Tiger Brown, the chief of police, and his closest friend to boot: "Whenever they had a cocktail together, they'd stroke each other's cheek and say, 'If you'll have another, I'll have another.' And whenever one went out, the other's eyes grew moist and he'd say, 'Whither thou goest, I will go too.' "

The dramatic situation arises when Macheath goes too far in following the bourgeois way of life and seeks Polly, Peachum's only daughter, in marriage. This is immoral, is the immediate reaction of the truly loving father. In cooperation with other whores, Peachum manages to have Macheath arrested and sentenced to death. Before his arrest, Macheath appoints Polly as the head of the organization and asks her to send all the profits to a banking house in Manchester. "It's only a question of weeks before I switch to banking exclusively. It's safer as well as more profitable." In his death cell, and after going through the company's books with his partner, chief of police Tiger Brown, Macheath delivers this indictment of his society:

> Ladies and Gentlemen. You see here the vanishing representative of a vanishing class. We bourgeois artisans, who work with honest jemmies on the cashboxes of small shopkeepers, are being swallowed up by large concerns backed by the banks. What is a picklock to a bank share? What is the burgling of a bank to the founding of a bank? What is the murder of a man to the employment of a man?

The Threepenny Opera was an immediate success everywhere, with the exception of Britain and the United States, if not for its subject matter and the poetic genius of the writer, then for the haunting music of Kurt Weill, Brecht's collaborator. In one of its memorable songs, the song of Pirate Jenny, the whore painfully expresses the fantasy of the woman dreaming of a ship with eight sails and fifty guns coming to take her to the shore of salvation after destroying the town and exterminating all her tormentors:

> Gentlemen, today you see me washing glasses
> And making up the beds for everyone,
> And you give me a penny and I thank you soon enough,
> And you see me dressed in rags in this raggedy hotel
> And you don't know who it is you're talking to –
> And you don't know who it is you're talking to ....
> But a day will come there'll be shouting in the harbour
> And you'll ask, "What is all that shouting for?"
> And you'll see me smiling as I do the glasses
> And you'll ask, "What is it she's smiling at?"
> And a ship, with eight sails
> And with fifty mounted cannons,
> Will be lying at the dock.
>
> They say, "Go dry your glasses, child,"
> And they toss me a penny,
> And I'll take up the penny, and the bed will be made –
> But this night no one at all will sleep in it,
> And they still won't know who I am,
> And they still won't know who I am ....

And this very night there will be thundering in the harbour
And they'll ask, "What's that thunder all about?"
And they'll see me standing there by the window
And they'll ask, "Why's her smile so mean?"
And a ship, with eight sails
And with fifty mounted cannons,
Will bombard the town.

Gentlemen, then there'll be no more of your laughing
For all of the walls will tumble down
And on the third day the city will be flattened –
Only a raggedy hotel will be spared a blow,
And they'll ask, "Who's so special that lives there?"
And then this night there'll be a din around the hotel
And they'll ask, "Why's this hotel being spared?"
And you'll see me stepping out at dawn
And you'll say, "She's the one who lives in there."
And a ship, with eight sails
And with fifty cannons,
Will run flags up its mast.

And towards noon a hundred men will land
And they'll walk in the shadows
And seize people in each doorway
And then chain them up and bring them all to me
And they'll ask me, "Which ones shall we kill?"
And this noon there'll be a stillness in the harbour
And they'll ask me, "Who will have to die?"
And then you'll hear me answer, "All of 'em!"
And when the heads roll, I'll say, "Hopp-la!"
And the ship, with eight sails
And with fifty mounted cannons,
Will vanish – with me.[3]

As the harlot became the symbol of the decay of society, the ship, the sail, the sea, the water, became symbols of her life and death in the imagery of Brecht and most of the other writers who portrayed her. The familiar method of suicide by drowning resorted to by fallen women inspired "The Bridge of Sighs", one of Thomas Hood's most popular poems in the last century. In the *Berliner Requiem*, written during the ascent of the National Socialists, Brecht included the poem "Vom Ertrunkenen Mädchen", about the drowned girl drifting from brooks to rivers, covered with seaweed and algae, surrounded by fishes swimming around her legs until her body decays and God gradually forgets her. She becomes carrion with the other carrion in the rivers.

Other songs in *The Threepenny Opera* include one by Mrs Peachum, the "Ballad of Sexual Submissiveness", and a duet by Macheath and Jenny, the "Ballad of the Pimp". The whores here are truly hard women and no ladies of the camelia. They have been cheated and downtrodden enough to know how far virtue can take a woman, or a man for that matter. Jenny, therefore, has no scruples at all in delivering Macheath over to the police for a bribe of ten shillings, notwithstanding all her sincere love for him. She loves him from all her heart, but never from all her stomach, so to speak.

Martin Esslin considers the Brechtian theatre an essentially negative theatre based on parody and denunciation and designed to arouse indignation and a realization of contradictions.[4] This assessment is obviously confined to his early plays, as the later works are full of positive characters who lead the community to salvation, but Brecht's earlier prostitutes definitely support Esslin's impression and point to a residue of pessimism from the German expressionist years.

Brecht's marxist understanding of morality is expressed more than adequately by Ginny Jenny:

> All you who say what neckline is decreed us
> And who decide when ogling is a sin
> Your prior obligation is to feed us
> When we've had lunch, your preaching can begin.
> You who insist upon your pleasure and our shame
> Take note of this one thing (for it is late):
> Your fine philosophy, good sirs, you may proclaim
> But till you feed us, right or wrong can wait!
> Or is it only those who have the money
> Can enter in the land of milk and honey?
> *Voice off*: What does a man live by?
> *Ginny Jenny*: What does a man live by? By resolutely ill-treating,
>   Cheating, beating, eating some other bloke!
>   A man can only live by absolutely
>   Forgetting he's a man like other folk!
> *Chorus off*: So, gentlemen, do not be taken in:
>   Men live exclusively by mortal sin.

To many people, *The Threepenny Opera* may seem just another piece of didactic literature full of poetic licence. Yet if such people recall to mind the underworld operation of the Mafia,[5] its monopoly of prostitution in many areas of the United States and its association with various public and political figures, the Brechtian world fades to a truly "middle-class idyll". The involvement of industry and high finance is just as well-documented. It is a common practice for many firms to resort to callgirls and nightclub hostesses to promote their businesses at the expense of the taxpayer.⁶ So much so that when the British Labour government of Harold Wilson abolished the free-for-all entertainment claims against income tax, the nightclub owners raised an outcry.

The complicity of the police in whoredom comes to light from time to time in nearly all countries.⁷ Early in the 1880s, tsarist Russia was rocked by the discovery of the involvement of the police chiefs of Ronstadt and Nikolayev in the prostitution business of their respective areas. The involvement of the New York police in the prosperous trade of the "red-light district" is also well known.⁸ The Report of the *Pall Mall Gazette* speaks of similar experiences in London. The laws were also made so as to provide protection to the pimps (for weren't they property holders?) rather than the innocent victims or their guardians. In the mid-nineteenth century there was a notorious case of fourteen prostitutes whose ages ranged between twelve and fifteen. Their parents were not allowed by the police to interfere or recover the children whoring in front of their eyes, until the brothel-keeper was eventually apprehended for selling drink without a licence!

One of the serious factors which contributed to the increase in prostitution was the involvement of the beer and spirits manufacturers in this profession. The giant beer firms of Britain grew together with prostitution from the beginning of the nineteenth century when they invested vast sums in their business, which they ran on a semi-monopolistic basis. Whitbread served 308 publicans in 1810 with 82 per cent tied houses; Barclay Perkins served 477 publicans in 1811 with 55 per cent tied houses. The stiff competition between these houses inspired them to use women as attractions for trade and to provide, in some cases, special rooms for debauchery. These were called the brothel-beer houses.⁹ The following are the figures given by Henriques illustrating the strong relationship that existed in 1917:

Parish	Population	Public Houses	Brothels	Prostitutes
St Botolph	5265	961	60	300
St Leonard's	48930	7282	100	700
St Paul's	98550	1082	200	1000

The beer industry, it could be said, had a stake in the common whore. Meux & Co. resorted to corruption and deception to thwart all efforts to have the licences of the brothel-beer houses withdrawn. A police report on the subject is revealing: "the tenderness of the magistrate towards so much property as is known to be embarked in public houses, has always operated against their doing their duty ...."[10]

The brothel-beer house or, more correctly, the brothel-whisky house, became the setting for Brecht's next opera, *The Rise and Fall of the City of Mahagonny*.

The Threepenny Opera was first staged in Berlin on 31 August 1928, when Brecht was still nearer to nihilism than to socialism or marxism. In the following few months, things deteriorated in Germany to a level unprecedented in his lifetime. The number of unemployed swelled to five million workers and overflowed into the streets in great mass demonstrations. During one of these demonstrations, held on the occasion of the First of May, the police opened fire and killed twenty young people in a bloody massacre which the young dramatist witnessed himself. His friend, the socialist Fritz Sternberg, described the feelings of his companion: "When Brecht heard the shooting, and saw that human beings were being killed, he turned white, as I have never seen him before .... I believe it was this experience that was not least influential in bringing him closer and closer to the communists."[11] He hastened to ask his friend to provide him with marxist books to find out what it was all about. Brecht went to the shops and bought five copies of the *Communist Manifesto* and Engels's *Road to Socialism*. Throughout the troubled months of 1928-9, he regularly attended courses on marxist history and philosophy at the Marxist Workers' College in Berlin. On 9 March 1930, *The Rise and Fall of the City of Mahagonny* was presented to the public.

When the police were mowing down the defenceless demonstrators, Hitler's National Socialists, dressed in brown shirts, were clamouring for the murder of all socialist traitors. Brecht used Mahagonny as a descriptive name of the colour of their shirts. Berlin, the city he loved and detested, the centre of German capitalism, he baptized as the City of Mahagonny. Yet it was not Berlin which became the scene of his new opera, but America. A group of people halt halfway to the goldmines and decide to set up a new city which will serve as a gathering centre for all the incoming gold. They call the city Mahagonny, and the capitalist motto of everyone for himself – "Nothing barred" – is adopted as its slogan. At the Sign of the Rich Man, Mrs Begbick establishes her brothel-whisky house, and her customers sing the song of the people of Mahagonny:

First, remember, comes your belly,
Then the whoring act.

Paul Ackerman spends all his money on his sweetheart, the whore Jenny, who, as in *The Threepenny Opera*, is again sincerely fond of her man. Paul is arrested for failing to pay the bill – "You are as good as dead." Mrs Begbick asks Jenny whether she couldn't help him out. Jenny, who is ready to devote body and soul to her beloved, stops short of lending him money. "Ridiculous!" she says. "What will be asked of us girls next?" And she sings this song, in which didacticism is so superbly matched with the score:

> As you make your bed you must lie there
> And no one will care what you do
> And if someone should kick then it's me, sir.
> And if someone gets kicked it will be you.

Jenny warns her listeners against the hardships of poverty and love. "I love you" is not hard to say, she goes on, but you grow older every day; you cannot start your life again through love; you have to use your short time on earth.

At Paul's trial, his judge is none other than the same brothel-keeper, the prosecutor is her partner. The public sit bored, reading their newspapers as the prosecution lists his various crimes until his defaulting on the bill is mentioned. They are suddenly alerted. "He's got no cash!" the chorus whispers in shock. For various crimes, including disturbing peace and order, the seduction of an innocent girl, the murder of a man in Alaska and the singing of a cheerful song at a time of trouble, Paul gets prison sentences, but for failing to settle his bill he is sentenced to death.

The Rise and Fall of the City of Mahagonny is saturated with a feeling of doom. It is a capitalist black mass, in Ewen's phrase. The opera begins with an approaching hurricane destroying one town after another but, with a bit of luck, missing Mahagonny. Yet the rumbling of the hurricane continues throughout the story, a feature which distinguishes this opera from the lighter and gayer *Threepenny Opera*. The ending also points to Brecht's conversion to a sterner look at the society of his time. Macheath was to hang on coronation day, but because of the occasion a messenger from the new monarch arrives announcing a reprieve. If only there was always a messenger from the king when someone is in trouble, the play says. In the city of Mahagonny there is no king and no king's messenger. Paul meets his certain death. The unhappy people of Mahagonny go out into the streets demonstrating with placards saying: "For Life and not for Death", "For Love and not for Hate". Kurt Weill now invokes

Jenny's tune, "As you make your bed, you must lie there", and puts it this time in the mouths of the masses rising defiantly:

> And if someone should kick then it's me, sir,
> And if someone gets kicked it will be you!

The opera reaches its great finale with the chilling death march "Nothing you can do will help a dead man". Before Paul's execution, Jenny visits him in prison and they sing a duet about love and its impossibility in the loveless world around them. This theme recurs in many places in Brecht's works and flows over into his dramatic technique. People are born good and beautiful, but the pressure of the evil world around them overcomes this inner goodness and makes them no better than beasts. They are "alienated" from themselves and begin accordingly to accept things which are neither good nor valid. The dramatist's job is to shake them out of their perverted ways of thinking and detach them from their emotional chains. The prostitute is the best illustration of this alienation process, which formed the core of Karl Marx's sociological philosophy. She is truly the woman with the heart of gold turned into the woman with the heart of rust. In *The Good Woman of Setzuan*, we shall see how Brecht had to put both hearts in the bosom of the same whore and let them operate alternately.

This dual psychology is evident in many of his works. We have seen how the rich landowner in *Puntila* alternates between the kind and benevolent gentleman when drunk and the ruthless employer when sober. The device of the split personality is used once more in *The Seven Deadly Sins*, the last play in which Brecht collaborated with Kurt Weill, produced in Paris in 1933. There the heroine, Anna, has two completely different personalities: Anna 1, a practical down-to-earth harlot, and Anna 2, a romantic woman ever disposed to charity and love. Anna tries to help her family by earning some income from dancing, but the public is not interested in ballet and high art. Anna is forced into prostituting herself, and succeeds in finding a rich man who gives her anything she wants. But whatever Anna 1 earns, Anna 2 squanders in an idealistic romance on a lover who exploits her. The personality conflict arises and Anna 1 scolds Anna 2 for her naivety and stupidity: "You can't give away love when it can be paid for. Love for the sake of love is lust."

The Rise and Fall of the City of Mahagonny had understandably aroused the anger of the National Socialists, who needed no one to tell them that the parody was not about America but about Germany – about themselves. They also recognized the different spirits of *The Threepenny Opera*, which they had received with some mild amusement, and of the *City of Mahagonny*, the city of the brown shirts. Alfred Polgar, the German critic who reviewed the first night, gave amusing accounts of the scuffling, whistling and clapping which accompanied the performance.[12] In one instance about a hundred Nazis had to be evicted. Their representatives in the parliament of Oldenburg demanded the cancellation of the scheduled performance of the opera, which was a "concoction of vile and immoral content". The right-wing critics were not moved by Kurt Weill's score or Bertolt Brecht's poetry and stamped the opera as nihilist and anarchic.

The Industrial Revolution did not fail to place its imprint on the technique of prostitution. The galvanization of rubber helped not only to produce reasonably reliable male and female contraceptives, but also a wider range of perversion requisites and articles. Chemistry gradually made the quack aphrodisiacs of the past a reality accessible to many people. The nineteenth-century literature on sex and prostitution gave long lists of the contortions and apparatus introduced by modern science to the whorehouses. Mrs Berkely resorted to the skill of the mechanic to introduce what became known as Mrs Berkely's Horse, a device on which a man could lie and have a nude woman underneath him while receiving sadistic stimulation from above. Mrs Berkely bequeathed the horse to the nation in her will.

Yet the most characteristic development was the introduction of the "factory production line", in which the whore catered to a line of customers in a mechanical sequence whose sole virtue was speed. We are in the stage of industrial prostitution wherein it has become quite common for a single prostitute, as one survey put it,[13] to dole out sex to fifty clients in one evening. In another postwar survey by O'Callaghan,[14] we hear of one brothel in New York employing a thousand whores. This was theatrically staged in the City of Mahagonny. At the Sign of the Rich Man, Mrs Begbick stands outside the whore's room instructing a queue of customers to get ready, spit out their chewing-gum, see that their hands are not too dirty, waste only a few words, etc. The chorus of the queuing customers, with hands in their trousers, repeats her instructions after her and sing: "Love is an act where you don't need to linger. Fellows, be quicker." The sight of clients queuing for the same prostitute while the pimp shouts his hurrying up words is pretty familiar in a successful brothel, and the present writer had quite a few occasions to witness the spectacle in many cities.

To project the picture of industrialized prostitution, one has to contrast it with the old rustic whoring, completely forgotten now, as depicted by that expert on brothel life, Guy de Maupassant, in "Madame Tellier's Establishment". Maupassant starts his quaint story by reminding us that the awful picture of prostitution as it is known in towns does not exist in the country. Madame Tellier is a good woman from a respectable peasant family, and takes up procuration in a small rural town as she might have taken up millinery or dressmaking. One day, her clients find her house closed, with the notice: "Gone on account of Confirmation." They protest and shout at this let-down; one of them even wants to complain to the government.

At the small town of Eure, she and all her girls, whom she treats maternally, attend the Confirmation of her niece. The mayor gives his pew close to the choir to Madame, and the girls take the best seats in the church. The priest touches the heart of one of them with his sermon and she starts to sob and cry. The other girls, including a Jewess, join her. This bout of religious fervour infects the whole congregation, and the church is turned into a pandemonium of sobs and tears, whereupon the priest thanks Madame for bringing the blessings of God on his parishioners.

Rivet, Madame Tellier's brother, becomes fascinated by Rosa during the dinner party. He tries to ravish her, amidst the laughter and merriment of everybody except Madame, who orders him to behave himself. Back at her inn (she strongly objects to calling it a brothel), she orders wine and food for herself, the girls and the clients. They dance and celebrate well into the night, and every man takes a girl with him to bed "on the house". The personal touch, the homely atmosphere, the communal feeling, the relaxed psychology and the unhurried tempo of life are all destroyed by the capitalist dynamite of profit-making, the maximum of profit in the minimum of time, the motto of the burglar, the Quran of the city of Mahagonny.

5
Under Colonialism

Prostitution was not generally a serious problem in the Third World before the intrusion of Western colonialism. Most people there lived on agriculture, which encouraged early marriage and childbearing. For the rich, there was the system of concubinage and polygamy. Here and there some form of respectable prostitution was permitted for other sections of the urban population. In some places prostitutes were attached to the temple, or – as in India – to the courts. The rights of the Indian court prostitutes were clearly defined and generously protected in return for part of their income, which went to the king. They were all carefully trained and educated for the practice of their profession, and some of the respect and appreciation due to them is reflected in the *Kama Sutra*. The Buddhists accepted the fate of the prostitute as a punishment for a transgression in a former life.[1]

All this quaint and rustic form of harlotry, which continued well into the twentieth century, was destined to give way to the more virulent form of capitalist prostitution introduced by the European colonialists. In some parts of the Third World, as in Polynesia, the population was to be subjected to wholesale prostitution and endemic venereal diseases. In India the terrible conditions to which women were reduced by the colonial soldiers prompted the British Parliament in 1888 to send a departmental committee to investigate the practice of prostitution in the army camps where prostitutes were encouraged and allowed to live.

Imperialism necessitated the dispatch of a massive number of men in the form of soldiers, sailors, administrators and entrepreneurs to the colonial world, and the result was a tempting demand for the sexual services of the native women. In some places, the industrial social dislocation which encouraged prostitution in Europe was repeated in the colonies, and the colonialists went so far as to use prostitutes as a managerial weapon. In Ghana, for example, the factor used to descipline his African workers by taking away their common whore.[2] In other parts, prostitution was encouraged by the police as a good source of income and by the trading companies as a channel for the consumption of liquor and Western goods.

Since the turn of the century, prostitution has reflected the multinational character of world imperialism, and the global traffic of white slavery has become its feature. This aspect was carefully monitored by the League of Nations, and its report on the subject underlined very clearly the multinational operations of the network. Alexandria, Beirut, Saigon and Hong Kong were the main centres, and women of various nationalities were bought and sold and transported to the various markets and even stored in economic places like Hong Kong and Macao for future use. The women were always in debt to souteneurs living across the seas and were treated like any commodity. One dealer wrote to another: "Next time you should send no goods to Singapore until you have got my wire in Hong Kong. If I ask for two pieces of goods you should only send me two and by no means too many. If you send too many, you will surely sustain a loss."[3]

The tendency favoured the supply of Greek women to the Middle East, Iraqi women to India and Chinese women throughout the Far East. In Egypt the demand was seasonal and depended on the number of Europeans wintering in Alexandria. There were, however, 1,670 registered prostitutes in 1920 and 670 registered brothels in 1923.[4]

The postwar situation was surveyed by O'Callaghan, and his findings leave us in little doubt as to the connection between colonialism and prostitution in the Third World. He described the profession in terms of international syndicates into which the Mafia had recently moved. The centre of this commerce was Tangiers, but the syndicates moved their activities to Beirut following the independence of Morocco in 1956. In Africa, the worst spots used to be the Portuguese colonies where white men from South Africa and Rhodesia were in the habit of seeking illicit sex with black girls.[5] Prostitution, however, went into decline soon after the independence of Tanzania, Morocco, Algeria and Tunisia. One of the interesting stories is the account of an episode related to an ex-SS German officer who stayed behind in Libya and turned to trading in Arab girls. He had his own aircraft to transport the women and made millions of pounds within a very short time.

The Middle East witnessed another chapter of colonial prostitution in the lands occupied by Israel after the 1967 war. In a letter addressed in 1970 by Professor Amitay Ben Yena of Jerusalem University to the American Left, under the title "What does Israel do to its Palestinians?", the writer speaks of the worst cases of prostitution in the world:

> Sometimes girls and boys cannot obtain work even in the citrus plantations, with wages nearly zero. There is no place for all the children in carpet-making. Hunger takes its toll and the revolver helps to remove such scruples that stomachs do not remove. Young children, male and female, sometimes of the same age as in the citrus plantation, that is ten years old – for some people have a superstition that cohabitation with the very young invigorates sexually – are auctioned, bargained and boasted about.

During the war in Vietnam, Saigon became a flourishing centre for local prostitutes catering to the American soldiers, so much so that on the first day following the fall of Saigon, the communist government proclaimed a ban on all nightclubs, dancehalls and brothels, and embarked soon after on tackling the problem of dealing with the army of Vietnamese prostitutes. The story of retraining them is documented in a number of films and reports.

A similar situation occurred in Algeria after independence. Indeed, the National Liberation Front issued a special order sentencing to death those who engaged in prostitution or procuring, a penalty which was carried out against a few offenders. One of the staunch Algerian fighters, Ali La Pointe, was himself a reformed pimp, and a number of notable women in the War of Liberation were ex-prostitutes. The story was unashamedly presented in the memorable film *The Battle of Algiers*.

It was almost symptomatic that whenever a colonial country gained independence, its native government had to face the problem of the "streets of shame" filled with bawdy nightclubs and brothels. At the same time, it is interesting to note that the colonialists rarely took any notice of the adverse social impact which they were making on the native population. The English sociologist H. Mayhew put the whole blame on the immorality and laziness of the profligate "barbarous nation" who lived without any ethical principles against the buying and selling of sex:

> The inhabitants of some islands and the shores of bay and roadsteads, have discovered that in prostituting their women to the crews of trading ships, they have a readier means of subsistence than was offered by their former industry. This has produced a frightful system of vicious commerce which still prevails to a great extent in the Pacific, as well as in New Zealand and parts of Africa.[6]

Referring to the numerous illegitimate children left by the British soldiers in India, he thought that "the immorality of the Hindoos, as far as it extended, was encouraged by their religion", and it was a blessing to see them develop "under the benevolent rule of the Company, a change which is perfectly wonderful to contemplate".[7] Dr Acton, on the other hand, recommended colonization and the dispatch of prostitutes to the colonies as a way of getting rid of prostitution in England.

The intelligentsia of the colonial world saw things quite differently. The young women who were seduced and corrupted by the colonialists and the half-caste children with blue eyes and white skin were there for them to see. So were the strings of brothels, bars and nightclubs catering for the foreign sailors and soldiers on a mechanical mass-production basis with no love or kind words to exchange. This was not sex, marital or extramarital, as known to the indigenous people of the colonial world. When a mere poet and patriotic fighter, Léopold Senghor wrote commenting on the Western life of fornication as he witnessed it in the brothel-land of Manhattan:

> No mother's breast, but only nylon legs and breasts that have
>   no sweat nor smell,
> No tender word for there are no lips, only artificial hearts
>   paid for in hard cash.

Whatever Mayhew had said about the immorality of the "Hindoos", Mahatma Gandhi found no better word to describe Western civilization than "prostitution". To him, even the British Parliament was nothing but a prostitute "under the control of ministers who change from time to time"[8] like a harlot's clientele. Gandhi was in the habit of talking of "Mother India" as a woman desecrated by foreign imperialism.[9]

The identification of colonialism with prostitution found a different echo in a poem by the Palestinian writer and political activist Kamal Nasir entitled "The Bastard Reared by the British and the Americans". Nasir was a writer fully committed to the Palestinian cause and was eventually killed in an Israeli commando raid. His hatred for the Israeli occupation and colonization of Arab land overflowed in his poem and confused the total picture. Israel was both a bastard and a prostitute of the Anglo-Americans:

> Slaves of slaves, you intruders abhorred by heaven and earth,
> Laugh and joke, for in the slumber of life, bastards laugh and
>   are merry.

Whoredom and deceit are disgraced with a fight waged through women.
History's eyes look with agitation at a state built with
fornication and prostitution.
Ask the British how they deflowered her virgins and made them
a sacrifice.
Ask them how they all have a sickly appetite for her.
They set her up as a den for vice, ever increasing in pimping
and coquetry,
A state of harlotry with a womb ever ready for whoredom and sin,
Fathered illegitimately by America and aborted, a deformed babe.
This is her mother, where is the father?
Has he played the fickle and betrayed his love?
Ask me not about the bastard, many a father passed through
her abode.

Most Asian writers have dealt with the problem of the moral disintegration of their societies and their established ethics as a result of the intrusion of Western fornication. One of the early examples of such literature is "Hindu Grhastha", a short story written in 1901 by Lajjaram Sarma about a young Indian intellectual corrupted by Western education and reduced to a life of dissipation and amorous adventures in England. This theme was repeated in many Asian stories.

The Punjabi writer Iqbal Singh dealt with the impact of Western industry in his short story "When One Is In It".[10] Singh tried to project the unity of time, space, past, future and present in the moment of a harlot's pregnancy. "When one is in it, the unreal distinction between the past, the present and the future are automatically obliterated." The proletarian milieu is present in the picture of the unemployed men and women begging for work outside a cotton mill. Among them stands Mirnalui the prostitute, struggling to control her heaving stomach. Opposite her, in his limousine, sits the managing director of Messrs Khambatta & Khambatta Ltd., swallowing digestive pills to calm *his* stomach over the vexing question of whether his wife's mole is below or above her navel. The story is typical of Indian didactic literature. Mirnaliu could only find employment in the factory if she supplemented her work with free sex to the overseer. "Once one is in it, it doesn't matter how one betrays someone else's bitter anguish." As she bends forward to receive her first wages, she loses control over her convulsions and the mass of her vomit covers the entire register and files of Messrs Khambatta & Khambatta Ltd.

A wealth of literature dealing with the character of the prostitute and the theme of her profession flowed from the pens of Algerian writers as they fought against French colonization in culture as well as politics. In his novel *L'As*, the marxist writer Taher Ovettar portrays the whole situation of Algeria in the character of the rebellious hero L'As, the illegitimate child of a Muslim woman serving as a washerwoman for the French, her paltry affluence due less to her domestic work than to sexual services provided to the French as a sideline. So much so that she cannot even remember who was the father of L'As. He grows up to be a proper thug, thief, drunkard and dealer in hashish, so he is in and out of prison all the time until he is swept up by the events of the War of Liberation.

Obsessed with the virginity of their girls and the virtue of their women, the Arabs could indeed find nothing worse – not even death – than the fall of a woman. The prostitution of their womenfolk by the occupation armies represented for them all the ills that could hit their national pride. This was most economically and artistically presented in the famous trilogy of the Egyptian novelist Najib Mahfuz. The master of the contemporary Arabic novel shows his insight into the whole continuum of sex, love, sin and venality over a long period of time extending from the early national attempt to gain freedom during the First World War to the years of the third generation of Egyptian national struggle during the Second World War.

In his first novel, *Bayn al-Qasrain*, we meet Said Ahmad, a man typical of the respectable merchant class, conscious of his duties and keen at the same time on his earthly pleasures of the flesh. Like Brecht's Puntila, he has a split personality. Just as he is jovial, easygoing and generous to the point of extravagance outside his home, he is stern, mean and ill-tempered inside. "His interests in women and experience in fornication sharpened his suspicion of female behaviour." The novelist contrasts the modern form of prostitution with the old tradition. "Oh, Shaikh Mitwally," says Ahmad, "the harlots of today are only the concubines of yesterday whom Allah has allowed us to acquire and sell."

One outcome of his adventure with a fallen woman is his son Yassin. With the other son, Fahmi, by a second wife, the writer tries to give his readers a lesson in heredity. From their father they both inherit the weakness for women, but Yassin receives from his wanton mother the additional fault of irresponsibility and recklessness, whereas Fahmi inherits from his sedate mother the Platonic sense of love and romance.

The Said receives his first shock of frustration when the British forces bar the natives from visiting the pleasure house of Azbakia and monopolize the sources of fun and games for themselves. Then comes a curfew in answer to Egyptian hostile acts. From boredom and lack of anything else to do, Yassin starts to chase the chambermaid, and eventually seduces her while gun-carrying British soldiers are patrolling the street outside his house.

The romantic Fahmi falls in love with his neighbour Miriam and seeks to marry her, but his father does not consider her good enough for the family, and the lover can find no escape but to join the ranks of the revolution, dreaming all the time of the V-day when he will offer his heart and soul in marriage to Miriam. But Najib Mahfuz gives the girl a different fate. During the days of war and struggle, a British soldier seduces her and reduces her to a camp-follower. Dying of a bullet wound after a mass demonstration, the hapless Fahmi breathes his last, thinking of Miriam and her British seducer. Soon after, Britain yields to Egyptian demands and the country gains its formal independence whilst the fallen woman, the wanton mother of Yassin, yields her soul to her creator.

In the second novel, *Qasr al-Shawq*, we witness the proper mass-production prostitution of the twentieth century. Both Yassin and his father compete for women, and both fall in love with the courtesan Zannuba. Not knowing where to take her, the coach driver directs Yassin to that eternal setting of illicit love, the bank of the river. "All is well," he assures him. "Every night I bring here good couples like you and return all safe and sound ...." – "Don't speak the word Nile. It gives me the creeps!" Zannuba rebukes the driver.

Soon everybody is preoccupied with the declining health of Egypt's national leader, Sa'ad Zaghlul. In a stormy portentous night, Zaghlul dies and Yassin becomes a father. Zannuba, the reformed harlot, now Yassin's wife, delivers her first baby safely. The new Egypt is born out of yesterday's whoredom.

In *Qasr al-Shawq* the novelist contrasts modern prostitution, and its queues of men waiting for a short time, with the old prostitution of Said Ahmad's generation, the prostitution of the *hetaera* type, with music, song and dance in a relaxed and dignified atmosphere.

While waiting their turn, the two brothers Kamal and Yassin argue about sex. "The love of wine and women has nothing to do with corruption," Yassin maintains. "Am I a blasphemer? Are you a blasphemer? Were the caliphs blasphemers? Allah is forgiving and merciful." What is the difference between a wanton woman and virtuous woman? The harlot is more sincere in her love and would be more dedicated to her marital life, he argues.

A realist and a social writer, Mahfuz was astute enough not to trap himself in the Western problem of sexual sin, the inescapable fate of the fallen woman or the romantic idealism of the whore. In this he was true to the older traditions of the Middle East. In the third novel, *al-Sukkaria*, which brings us into the Second World War, we meet Zubaida, the ageing harlot with her flabby body and wrinkled face. She sells everything for a shot of cocaine. The Said sits with his friends playing dice: "Who will have the luck of Zannuba and who will have the luck of Zubaida?"

It is all a matter of Kismet, how things will turn out for the harlot. Although instructed by God to kill the adulterous woman and whip the sinful girl, middle-class Muslims did not in practice show the same eternal condemnation as their European counterparts in regard to the fallen woman. As far as the harlot is concerned, Allah seems to be more forgiving than the God of the Christian middle class. Zannuba proves to be a very successful wife and mother, and the profligate Said Ahmad dies in dignity in the arms of his wife, reciting the full Muslim prayer.

Yet poor Miriam, "the whore of the British", as they call her, could not be one of the lucky harlots. In the final political argument of the trilogy, one of the characters shouts: "Britain is our enemy No. 1." And poor Miriam has prostituted herself to this enemy. The God of heaven may forgive, but not the God of nationalism. On a night that echoes with the sounds of air-raid alarms, Kamal, the youngest brother, sees her in a nightclub frequented by the allied forces. "Like that she started with the British and like that she would end up with the British," he says, praying to God for a German bomb to wipe him out.

The trilogy is not the only instance in which Mahfuz involves himself in the character of the prostitute. He goes back to this theme time and time again. In a more outspoken and less authentic novel, *The Thief and the Dogs*, we meet the unfortunate Said Mahran, a young man driven by force of circumstances to robbery, but betrayed by his friend and accomplice to the police. After a spell in prison, he comes out to find his wife taken over by his friend. He turns to the local clergy for help, but there is no help from God to men like him. Then he turns to Alwan, once a revolutionary socialist whom Mahran served in his early life, but Alwan, now a successful and affluent journalist, does not want to know him. He is finally driven to murder, and the police set up a merciless hunt for him. The only person who stands by him to the bitter end is Nur, the common whore hailing from Cairo's poorest district. Nur is just another prostitute with a golden heart, but the writer is obviously less interested in her characterization than in exploiting her as a vehicle for projecting the utter decadence and ruthlessness of Egyptian society.

Arab writers and poets were invariably influenced by the romanticized image of the harlot of European literature. Dumas's *La Dame aux Camélias* was one of the early examples of French novels translated into Arabic and made into a film. The social commitment of Arab writers also made them far too susceptible to the easy notion that prostitution is simply due to poverty. One of the outstanding examples in this vein is the long poem "The Blind Prostitute" by Badr Shakir al-Sayyab, the Iraqi poet who exerted a tremendous influence on contemporary Arabic poetry. He wrote the poem when he was fully committed to the communist cause, and it shows many traces of his beliefs. Driven by hunger, the blind girl's peasant father gets killed while trying to steal some wheat, and the blind girl has to rely on the help of her neighbour Jasmin.

> And God, praise be to God, willed it
> That from far-off lands and seas
> Thousands of thousand men moved into Iraq
> To seduce out of all the thousand maidens,
> Out of all the thousand alleys,
> The baker's daughter, the hapless Jasmin.

The blind girl joins Jasmin in prostitution, but she is less fortunate with customers than her friend. Men seem to think that by losing her sight she lost her power of attraction.

> Come, drunkards, don't leave me starving to death.
> Life, after my death, is a disgrace.
> Have no worries. My blindness is no sign of respectability
>   or prudishness,
> I still know how to tune my laughter under my bosom
> And dance lazily while I take off my clothes.
> I know how to grasp the bed linen and throw back my head.
> I still know all that. Just try me, drunkards.
> Those who sleep with the brown Arab girl will not be sorry.
> Like the colour of wheat is the Arabian girl,
> Like the dawn breaking through the vine,
> Or like the Euphrates with its hues of earth and glow of gold.
> Don't leave me! I am the daughter of midday,
> I am the descendant of the conqueror, the mujahid and the
>   prophet.
> Arab am I. In me, as my father said,
> Flows the supreme blood of the Arabs.
> In the place of my disgrace in my body,

> In my humiliated breasts,
> Flows the blood of conquerors,
> Oh, men, come and desecrate it!
> For yesterday the soldiers from across the seas
> Like a mass of worms desecrated it.

"The Blind Prostitute" is certainly one of the best examples of a poet resorting to the image of the common whore in an hour of intense rage and disgust. No other symbol could serve the purpose better. Al-Sayyab was a very sensitive poet and deeply conscious of his country's plight under the yoke of imperialist control. In another poem, "The Brothel", he describes his country's capital in these words:

> A great brothel is Baghdad,
> The eyelashes of the harlot ticking away
> Like a clock on a wall
> In a waiting-room of a railway station.
> Oh, lump of corpse lying on the earth,
> With worms in waves of flame and silk.

A similar political outburst came from the pen of Mu'in Basisu in his *Tragedy of Che Guevara*. Although written clumsily by a poet of little consequence, the play was seen by packed audiences in Cairo. In it we meet the harlot in the person of Marina, the soothsayer who sleeps with the father-confessor and gets from him the information necessary for telling the fortunes of each villager:

> I am Marina,
> Your priest's mistress.
> Which of you don't know Marina?
> Which of you haven't slept with Marina?

Again the town is represented by the whore, the drunken whore holding her glass of wine. She tumbles over and falls in the street. People walk over her and soldiers empty their glasses in her face, until she is rescued melodramatically by Che Guevara.

In *Five Voices*, a novel by the Iraqi writer Ghaib Tu'ama Farman, the reader spends a great deal of time in Baghdad's brothel-land. There is a sense of doom as the US army helicopter takes the journalists on an inspection flight over the flood-bound city whilst the heart of the city throbs with the activities of its notorious brothels. There Sharif the poet holds long discussions with his prostitute girlfriend and tells her about the wonders of Europe, where women don't become prostitutes like her. The girl squanders her affection and care on her intellectual customer and hopes to marry him. But the middle-class young man spurns her and marries a university graduate like himself.

The impossible fate of the prostitute is illustrated also in Ahmad Abbas's short story "Radha". The Indian writer tackles the question of the traditional courtesan dancer and sexual artist. Hired to the Raja of Jalbur for 500 rupees a month, Radha falls in love with him and tries in vain to win his respect in matrimony. Under the influence of their English education, both story-writers seem to echo the social values of Victorian England.

With the liberation of the former colonies and dependent countries, the new nationalist and socialist leaders hastened in most cases to close the public brothels and chase out the common whore as a blemish staining the dignity and emancipation of the country. In liberated Vietnam, reform camps were opened for the re-education of the hordes of prostitutes left over by the GIs. Colonel Qaddafi of Libya went on attacking Muhammad Ali Street (Cairo's red-light district) as the symbol of decadent Egypt and called for its immediate closure. In his pursuit of this subject, the attempts of the present writer to visit areas traditionally known to accept organized prostitution were discouraged by the Algerian authorities, and the matter was simply brushed aside as the "work of imperialism". Regardless of the failure or success of this effort, there seems to be a marked decline now in the literary preoccupation of post-independence writers with the question of the harlot and her profession. Under the guidance of social realism and state patronage of the arts, members of the people's militia, female tractor drivers and heroic women of the national struggle are now the approved heroines of liberated Third World literature. To all intents and purposes, the prostitute seems to have lost the element of recognition even from her traditional patron, the artist, without gaining the promised redemption.

6

Black Women, White Men

Nowhere did the impact of colonialism on the social structure of native communities reveal itself more clearly than in the history of the black peoples. Again, the introduction of industrial and trading centres led to the same results as those which had occurred in Europe. In most of Africa, as elsewhere in the world, there were certain arrangements for sexual diversion. In addition to polygamy there were various forms of premarital free love and institutionalized prostitution. In many communities there was a public whore allocated by the chieftains and publicly initiated into the profession.[1] On the other hand, family cohesion was jealously guarded. All this traditional set-up was undermined by the intrusion of Western colonialism with its utter disregard of family requirements.

The fate of the black woman is closely connected with the story of slavery. Throughout the Middle Ages there was a scramble in which Asian and European slave merchants were competing for the capture, import and sale of blacks. The females were wanted for domestic service, slave-breeding, concubinage and prostitution. The women found it difficult to distinguish between the various roles expected of them, and very often had to perform all these roles. In the Caribbean, the imported blacks were treated in the same way as cattle, encouraged to mate and produce more slaves. Marriage was not allowed for them and sexual potency was considered a mark of value in the male slave. As a result of this, the distinction between marriage and fornication was blurred and the legitimacy or illegitimacy of a child mattered very little.

The slave woman, of course, was completely at the sexual disposal of her master and it was commonplace for European men in the West Indies to keep coloured mistresses. The women themselves were willing to have sexual intercourse with white men because of the hope of freedom promised by the birth of a child from such unions. So it is not very surprising to find sex and sexual energy used in black and Caribbean literature as indicators for freedom and liberation. One may also observe an overlap in attitudes to legitimate and illegitimate love and moral and immoral earnings. Influenced by marxism and expressionism, the Harlem school of black American writers reacted strongly against the latter-day attempt to endow Negroes with respectability and God-fearing piety. In Claude McKay's novel *Banjo*, Christianity and sexual purity cloak colonialism and bawdiness.[2]

There were more reasons for the slave woman to be sexually acquiescent. For one thing, there was the whip if she dared reject the advances of her master. If freed, she could have little prospect of marriage, because no white man would marry a black woman and to take a black husband would only relegate her to her former state of slavery. The result of the mixed intercourse was the birth of "mulatto" children; and a mulatto girl, because of her bronze colour and often interesting features, became in great demand, which in turn increased the pressure of prostitution on her. White masters used to force their female slaves to sleep with white men to produce the new more profitable product.[3]

After the abolition of slavery, middle-class Christian values started to take root in the black camp in terms of the respectability and good behaviour expected by whites. Many black writers responded positively towards this new trend and wrote of black heroes and heroines rising up to the standard of puritan virtues and Anglo-Saxon ideals. Soon, such expectations were disappointed as the abolition of slavery was shown to be only a legal arrangement and the road to complete equality was far too long. A new school of black writers thus evolved around the rejection of the entire morality of the white man. The most prominent spokesman of this new trend was the Jamaican-born Claude McKay, poet, journalist and novelist. He called for the rejection of the industrial life which had led black people into an abnormal existence based on bourgeois values. McKay saw black sex in terms of purity, as contrasted with Christian purity in terms of inhibitions.[4] The tragic existence of black Americans was epitomized for him in Harlem, with all its sordid life. In "Home to Harlem" he expressed his contempt in style and subject matter for everything that savoured of bourgeois respectability. His poem "Harlem Shadows" portrays the life of the black street-walker:

I hear the halting footsteps of a lass
In Negro Harlem when the night lets fall
Its veil. I see the shapes of girls who pass
To bend and barter at desire's call ....

Through the long night ...
The dusky, half-clad girl of tired feet
Are trudging, thinly shod, from street to street.
Ah, stern, harsh world, that is the wretched way
Of poverty, dishonour and disgrace,
Has pushed the timid little feet of clay,
The sacred brown feet of my fallen race!
Ah, heart of me, the weary, weary feet,
In Harlem wandering from street to street.

In Africa, the conditions of the black race deteriorated under the rule of the white man. The main factor in this respect was the dislocation which affected the old village community and disturbed the natural balance between males and females. A British Royal Commission noted, for example, that about half of the able-bodied men of Basutoland were away working as labourers in South Africa and that their employers paid them their wages and travel expenses as single men only.[5] Another report spoke of some 30 to 60 per cent of able-bodied men drawn away at one time or another in Central Africa with no compensating social measures adopted, and concluded: "the family-community is threatened with complete dissolution".[6] In most cases the migration of such men was forced on them by the Belgian and Portuguese colonial administration.

In the mining and industrial centres, the congregation of men of all races and nationalities, Europeans, Indians, Chinese and Africans, aroused a heavy demand for the sexual services of women, who happened to live also under extreme poverty. In *The Dispossessed*, L. Longmore gives a valuable account of the conditions which led to prostitution among Bantu women, concluding that poverty was the main cause for the practice – "No doubt many women successfully, though surreptitiously, combined all four roles of being simultaneously wife, mother, prostitute and extra breadwinner for the household."[7] Indeed, many wives had no reason to conceal the fact, as the economic pressure forced fathers and husbands to encourage their daughters and spouses to go out for prostitution. One of the causes of the persistent poverty was that the Africans were usually paid as Africans, but were required to pay as Europeans when they went shopping, and were forced to live beyond their means.

In some industrial estates in parts of Africa, prostitution was carried out in the back yards of the premises, with men queuing for a chance at pitiful prices, and those who could pay extra fees allowed to jump the queue. These "brothels" – which had two different departments, one for white and one for black customers – were often linked with the public houses, and the picture of drunkenness, disorder, robbery and venality was complete.

There seemed to be almost a white conspiracy to eradicate the purity of the African. While men were taken to work as single people, without their wives, the women were taken into domestic service, without their husbands being allowed to live with them. The appetite for destroying the purity of the black girl is further evidenced by the desire of the Europeans to purchase young girls, often from the local school, to use them in their houses as chambermaids and concubines. According to O'Callaghan, some white masters had as many as fifty such girls at their command,[8] and child prostitution was widespread throughout West Africa. In Beira, Mozambique, there were special brothels provided for government officials with harlots in their early puberty. There is even evidence that missionaries encouraged girls to prostitute themselves to white men.[9]

This state of things was first exposed in literary form by liberal and Christian-minded Europeans like Alan Paton with his classic novel *Cry, the Beloved Country*, first published in 1948. The novel deals with the fate of a Zulu family in the midst of this social dislocation when the soil cannot keep them any more. There is sickness in the land, the grass disappears, weeds run from hill to valley and from valley to hill, and it becomes a land of old men and women. The tribe is broken, the house broken, the men broken, they all go away and never come back, never write back. The young girls go too, and forget their customs and live loosely.

When he wrote his novel, Paton was a lecturer in South Africa and became a head of a reformatory and a leading figure in the Liberal Party. Like many members of the white liberal camp, his inspiration was a religious one. *Cry, the Beloved Country* therefore reflects a Christian ethic and a Christian social understanding.

We first meet the Reverend Stephen Kumbalo receiving a letter informing him that his sister Gertrude is very ill in Johannesburg, where she has gone with her child looking for her missing husband. Her husband was supposed to have gone to work in the mines, but never came back when his employment ended. "When people go to Johannesburg, they do not come back," says Mrs Kumbalo. The parson is therefore set to go and search for his sick sister. "But it is not that kind of sickness. It is another," he is told: "She lives in Claremont ... you can see the liquor running in the streets." After a long search Stephen Kumbalo discovers the whereabouts of Gertrude in one of Johannesburg's seedy brothels, but she is adamant not to leave with him. "I am a bad woman," she cries. The man of God now reassures her of God's infinite mercy and forgiveness. In the middle of the whoring chamber, both the prostitute and her saviour fall in prayer (this scene was omitted in the film version of the story). Gertrude realizes full well that her return to a normal respectable life is out of the question; and, having delivered her son to the good care of her brother, she makes her retreat to a convent.

Cry, the Beloved Country served as an inspiration for many stories and novels written by white and black writers alike, dealing with the loss of an African woman's virtue in the squalid urban centres of Africa as a result of the rural migration to the towns. Time and time again we encounter the African nightclub girl and street-walker hailing from the distant villages.

In *Turbott Wolfe* by the South African-born William Plomer, published in 1926, we find a novel with a different approach to the issue of African prostitution. The writer shows his European romanticism and fauvist influences by idolizing the "natural" woman and an idealized notion of the "primitive". The hero, an artist-shopkeeper under the spell of Paul Gauguin, with his right foot firmly placed on a money bag marked in green ink "8% interest charged on overdue accounts" and a left foot balancing on a bag of other people's dirty washing, falls in love with Nhliziyambi, an African woman fit to be "the wife of an ambassador".

> She was a fine rare savage of a type you will find nowhere now: it has been killed by the missions, the poor whites and the towns .... The missionaries brought them the sacrament, but I could give you more than one instance where they brought them syphilis too.

Shortly before meeting this noble savage, the hero gets involved with a white whore, Cossie van Honk, locally nicknamed the Aucampstroom wife. This name is a guide to her profession, as she is a wife for the whole group.

> She wasn't an ordinary prostitute. She was as much a public institution as the town hall. In the warm dusk, I saw that her wrinkled face was ghastly with cheap powder, heavy with paint, panting violently. A hideous mask. She stank of scent and in the quiet dark street I heard the patter of her feet and the rustling of her silks, as she went deliberately and purposefully about her business with a cachou on her tongue. The greatest obscenity was that in the daytime she was a certified midwife.

Having met both women, he makes up his mind to extricate himself from white society and stay with the blacks in Lemburland, but the visions of Cossie van Honk go on haunting him wherever he finds himself face to face with the ugly deeds of the white race. Labelled by the whites as a nigger-kisser, he is eventually served notice to leave the area. On his way out he finds himself walking in the street where the Aucampstroom wife used to walk "with a hard heart and a soft body". As he passes towards the railway station, he hears laughter at a piano. It is Cossie singing "You Called Me Baby Doll a Year Ago".

Black African writers had no didactic tradition rooted in their literature, unlike writers in India or China; their treatment of the prostitution theme was often more of a statement than a commentary. And in most cases they have come into their own after the attainment of self-government, when the struggle against colonialism was no longer a burning issue. Their work has been more concerned with the corrupt rulers and leaders who rose to office after independence than with the misdeeds of the white colonialists or the exploitation of European imperialism. The prostitute has become an indictment of the new native bourgeoisie, the bureaucracy, the ruling class, the new breed of black white man, the urban squalid existence of nightclubs, dancehalls and general corruption and decay. Sometimes the writer is simply fascinated by the character of the black whore and indulges in portraying her life, thoughts and looks.

The young Ugandan novelist Okello Oculi gives us one example in *The Prostitute*, a story which makes a limited attempt to deal with the problem of the harlot and the social background of her life, though when he goes on to portray her thoughts and feelings they seem to be more like his own thoughts about a variety of subjects, not necessarily related to the story of prostitution. In the first chapter Oculi gives an evocative description of the squalor engulfing the African harlot, the brown stagnant water, the urine, pus and vomit. The seedy sexual existence is conveyed in this liquid, smelly environment. The white man makes his appearance:

> She remembered too those black-red eyes of her white customers. She preferred them for convenience. They pay more. They are frank (call it vulgar, if you like) and talk straight business, just the way the hunger inside her and the smell of the urine and the rent of the room she hires talk straight and ruthlessly to her. She remembers the monkey-like hair on their chests and on their arms, their wrinkled skins remind her now of the patches around the ends of gorillas. "Darling ... eh, you dear ... take forty, OK ... eh, friend ... want to sleep ... baby ... come on!" The sounds of the stock market at boom operation, minus the roars and screams

of the teenagers said to have been caught into record somewhere in the homes of these pink-red men. The jukebox too is made from there. All the vulgarity in the whole thing is dim, new in her mind. She is dead to such feelings now. It had all started as a novelty. Sleeping with a white or pink-skinned person! It felt awkward. Revolting. But what were they like ... are they also like men ... do they know anything like our men? They have children, but maybe they do some strange things. These people are strange, her parents had always said. These men had sold people for money and they kill people by bursting them up with big fires that explode. They like such violent deaths. Such people .... Ah! If she went with one she may never see the sun again the next day. These fears and confused thoughts of curiosity, despising, doubt and fear had always filled her about these people when she first came into these things. But a friend of hers had insisted once, pulled her and pushed her into a car from behind and they had travelled together with two of these men who wanted them. From then on she had become used. Today all those beers she had drunk from them are like the wreaths to her pride's graveyard, her pride which existed once.

Thus the black woman is seduced, or raped, by the white colonialist in the back of his car and the way is opened for her towards the jukebox whorehouses.

The subject of the prostitute was rarely, if at all, handled by female writers anywhere in the world. From Ghana, however, Ama Ata Aidoo, dramatist and short-story writer, showed her courage by tackling exactly this subject. Her theme is the usual one of the unfortunate girl who falls into prostitution as a result of moving from country into town. In "Something to Talk About on the Way to the Funeral", Ama Ata Aidoo tells the story of Auntie Araba, who is sent to town by her family to look for employment, only to find herself made pregnant in a short time by one of the refined barristers she works for.

The evil effect of urban life on the traditional rural communities continued after independence with only one difference: the national ruling élite took the place of the former European rulers. Ama Ata Aidoo projects this development in her short story "For Whom Things Did Not Change". One of the men speaks of the new black "masters" who are bedding the young girls just as the white masters used to do. In reply, his wife says that this is always the situation when an intruder comes, takes over your land and does all the things which a good man should not do. When you recover your land eventually, you cannot but continue on his ways of destruction.

Being a dramatist as well as a storyteller, Aidoo often writes her story in dialogue form with a great deal of naturalistic African idiom. In "The Cutting of a Drink" we are told of young Mansa, who is supposed to have married a rich man in the city. Not hearing any more about her, the family decide to send her brother to look for her. He finds her in a dancehall together with three other prostitutes picking up men and dancing "white man's dances".

"Young women, is this the work you do?"
"And who are you to ask me such a question? I say, who are you? Let me tell you that any kind of work is work, you villager!"

In a piece reminiscent of Jean Genet's *The Balcony*, Okot p'Bitek, poet, artist and sociologist, introduces us to the character of the prostitute in the "Song of Malaya". The poem is dedicated to the memory of the African leader Patrice Lumumba, and puts the case of the whore in the first person singular. Her services are sought by everybody – the black bishops, members of parliament, village teachers, police officers, etc. It is a strongly worded attack on the newly set up African establishment. Harsh, lusty and outspoken, the whore lashes out at the hypocrisy and cant of the rising bourgeoisie:

Tell me, you men
Who split open
The opok tree
And scoop out the honey
With your bare hands
Fearing not the bees ...

Do you take
Some of the honey
To your wives?

Do they also
Enjoy the sweet fruits
Of your adventures?

You presidents, ministers,
Liberators of Africa,
You heroes,
You who defeated colonialism
And imperialism

True sons of Africa
Brave fighters against
Corruption and decay
You revolutionaries ...

Where are the advisers
The experts and mercenaries

> Can we not free Africa
> From this one pest?

The poet gives the answer in the negative. There is no way for the eradication of this vice from the face of Africa, because it has now become part of African life. Therefore:

> Sister prostitutes
> Wherever you are,
> Wealth and health
> To us all.

The most outstanding piece in African written literature dealing with prostitution is undoubtedly *Jagua Nana* by the Nigerian novelist Cyprian Ekwensi, first published in 1961 and later translated into many European languages. The social involvement of this writer and his frequent treatment of the lower strata of African society prompted some critics to call him the Charles Dickens of Africa. *Jagua Nana*, set against a panorama of Nigerian life and written with an epic sweep, reveals a woman with the same reckless nature and dissatisfied and restless soul as her counterpart in Zola's novel. She is the archetypal prostitute, vain but good-natured and tender. Strangely enough, Ekwensi confirmed that he had never heard of Zola's Nana:

> After *Jagua* was published I was surprised to hear of Zola's *Nana*. I have still not been able to read it, and in fact have not tried. Jagua in the 1950s in West Africa meant everything that was good and worth aspiring to. The word came from a corruption of the British car Jaguar – which at that time signified success, especially among the "Been-tos", those who had had a British education. Nana is simply a name more commonly found in the Gold Coast [Ghana] than in Nigeria though not exclusive to Ghana. Since I did not read Zola, I could not have intended *Jagua Nana* as an African *Nana*.[10]

Ekwensi's Nana starts her career with a broken marriage. Her husband is drawn away from her by the world of the new money-making industry. Left to her own devices, she moves to Lagos in search of work, but the only work she can find is through a procurer who takes her to an English businessman. Thus seduced by the white colonialists, Jagua Nana eventually drifts to the "super sex market" of the Tropicana Club, where European bank managers, oil men, shipping agents, brewers of beer, pumpers of swamp water, building contractors, healers of the flesh, German, English, Dutch,

Americans, Nigerians and Ghanaians congregate in the common quest for diversion.

Jagua Nana falls in love with a young man, and the pursuit of her lover brings her into the midst of Nigerian tribal politics. In that country of endemic strife, she visits the two villages of Bagana and Krinameh, locked in a futile family feud which puts a halt to all progress in the area. Chief Ofubara of Krinameh speaks to her of the development, education and social work needed by his people: "We are all Africans and we must come together. There is no time for petty squabbles." But pride prevents this coming together, and the woman who has lost her pride and lived with the cosmopolitan spirit of the prostitute, above all national barriers, sees the stupidity of tribal and national rancour:

> "An' you promise to give me wardrobe. An' I know dat if ready to give me money, it will be something' ... but I don' ask you for all dat. I jus ask you to come with me to Bagana an' shake hand with uncle Namme. Den you two kin talk. Lissen, Chief Ofubara. Your country people, dem suffer because of dis foolish proud. So I beg you for my sake. Just now you talk with me. You say you wan' unity. Well, I goin' to give you de chance to get unity ...."

She gets down and unbuttons her skirt; she is wearing silk undergarments frilled with fine lace. Like that, she struts about the room in her high heels and juts out her hips.

> He took her to bed and she gave herself with an abandon calculated to shock and delight him. The feigned noises, practised over the years, the carefully punctuated sighs and cries of pain, the sudden flexing of thighs and neck ... all those she performed with a precision which surprised herself. It was a long time since she had played her true role.

Yet her art is not the only factor which inflames the man's desire. It is the first time, Ekwensi emphasizes, that Chief Ofubara has experienced the sensation of the African woman as an equal partner, and the experience makes the master her slave, ready to obey her maddest whims. (But is she actually an equal partner? She is only pretending, like everyone in the emergent nations.) The following day, Jagua leads the chief to the palace of Chief Namme and peace is made amidst the frenzied rejoicing of the population. The door is opened for the development of the area, trade flourishes, schools and clinics are opened. With all the bloody conflicts which have rocked West Africa, one cannot help wishing there were more Jaguas and Nanas in that part of the world.

In pursuit of another lover, Jagua finds herself once more in the midst of politics. The unscrupulous leader of the OP2 Party, Uncle Taiwo, wants her to help him win the votes of women. "Tell them anything you like, no one is going to remember electioneering promises," he assures her. She is the right tool for the right job, for who could outstrip the professional politicians in improvising lies better than the professional prostitute? In the middle of the market squalor, and by the side of the rubbish dump and running drain, Jagua Nana delivers one of the most effective speeches ever concocted by an African leader. Yet Uncle Taiwo's campaign misfires. He is soon involved in the murder of his opponent, a former lover of Jagua, and he is in turn murdered by the opposite camp, leaving the stolen funds of his party in his mistress's custody. Jagua sends the money to the villages of Ofubara and Krinameh for the schooling of children.

Although Jagua Nana loses her only child during her adventures, she does not suffer from the Judeo-Christian handicap and finds her own salvation and self-respect in the end. This was considered as a fault by Eustace Palmer, the noted critic of African literature: "Ekwensi seems to try to persuade the reader to share his captivation with her. There is very little criticism, either of her or of the threat which the dangerous Lagos underworld presents to civilized standards."[11] Indeed, the novelist does not see anything wrong with the progress of Nana's life and wonders about the question of her fall: "Fallen from what? She chose not to have a husband. That is not 'falling'. It is 'independence'. That is how it is regarded by her."[12]

Ekwensi seems to give support to an attitude shared by other black writers, as was pointed out at the beginning of this chapter, namely that free love equals freedom, in the political and economic sense. *Jagua Nana*, however, suffers as a novel from other defects, and the behaviour of the heroine remains bewildering. But the work as a whole falls within the category of African literature portraying the underworld life of industrial and commercial cities as an open trap for the original virtue and innocence of Africa.

7

The Woman with the Heart of Gold

One of the basic changes in subject matter introduced by nineteenth-century writers and artists was the switch of emphasis from aristocratic heroes to ordinary common folk, from Velázquez's princely figures to Daumier's blackened proletarian faces. Weavers and miners, beggars and unemployed workers, dustmen and flowergirls became the new heroes and heroines, but none could surpass the prostitute as the prize subject for the avant-garde of the period. She was a character well suited to the romantic inclination of the writers: there was adventure in her, the element of mystery and the unknown; she opened the door to a love of torment *par excellence*; she was of the people and smelt of country pollen. Her rebirth and glorification offered the new writers the chance of revolt against the past, the defiance of the accepted, and the opportunity to look modern and be "with it". Russian Utopian writers projected her as the champion who would lead the proletarian revolution of the future, and intellectuals of the French Revolution hastened to enthrone a harlot as "The Supreme Being".

But there was more in the idolization of the whore than mere romantic fashion. The bourgeoisie needed her, but they wanted her without her disadvantages. They wanted a quiet, meek and peace-loving whore. A selfless and good-hearted woman suited their book better. They learned that the best way to get self-sacrifice from worker, soldier or harlot was to instil this spirit in them by suggestion. The songs and poems about the contented peasant, the hard-working weaver and the fearless soldier, all ready to starve and die in the service of king and country, were now extended to include the harlot.

Guy de Maupassant,[1] who showed the most profound appreciation of the relationship between the prostitute and society, hit the jackpot in this respect as well. His whore, Boule de Suif, is travelling in a stagecoach with eight other passengers, "the representatives of revenued society, serene in the consciousness of its strength – honest, well-to-do people possessed of religion and principles". They are a fair cross-section of the establishment: a wine merchant, a cotton manufacturer, an aristocratic count, their wives – and two nuns. The revenued members of society look down on this common woman and drive her to tears with their contempt. As expected the women are harder on her, "for legalized love always takes a high hand with her unlicensed sister". The men put her in her place by talking about the selling and buying of their valuable properties, now and then casting a look at the woman who only sells her body.

It is during the Franco-Prussian war, and a German officer stops the coach at Totes. Of all the female passengers, he picks, of course, the prettiest – the whore. Boule refuses to indulge his desire and the officer delays the coach as long as she resists. Now the men of religion and principle go down on their knees to her, with their wives and the two nuns, and appeal to her in the name of patriotism and Christianity to sleep with the enemy. France expects it of her. God has created her for this noble task. They remind her of the numerous saints and great women of history who dedicated their sexual organs to the service of man and God. "To hear them you would have finally come to the conclusion that woman's sole mission here below was to sacrifice her person, to abandon herself continually to the caprices of the warrior." Boule eventually yields and goes upstairs. Down below, the merchants, manufacturers, wives and nuns sit at the table and celebrate with champagne. Every now and then, one of them shouts "Silence", looks up at the ceiling, listens attentively and then beams with pleasure – "It is all right."

The idealization of the prostitute was the first step towards the recognition of prostitution and the rationalization of the chaotic service. It is no wonder to find the idealizer of the whore often in the person of the reformer of her profession. One of the early reformers in this field was Alexandre Dumas the younger, who wrote a tract on the sanctity of marriage and the dangers of fornication. This work of his is hardly known, but he will be ever remembered for his novel *La Dame aux Camélias*, which stirred the French public in 1848 and placed one of the first milestones along the road of rehabilitating the prostitute in literature. The story of the fallen woman who reciprocates a young man's love only to banish him under pressure from his family and in concern for his future, then dies of a broken heart and tuberculosis, is all too well known. It was made into a play in 1852, sung to the score of Verdi in 1853, filmed many times and translated into all the major languages. *La Dame aux Camélias* has probably sent more tears down the cheeks of the middle class than all the wars that were fought on their behalf since the first publication of the novel, a fact which must make Aristotle purr in his grave as he sees so much "catharsis" brought about by pity.

Nevertheless, this sentimental journey of Dumas did not please the censor, who misunderstood the ultimate message of the story. The play version was refused a licence by the Lord Chamberlain in England. George Henry Lewes (who took George Eliot for his mistress) condemned the innocent novel as "this unhealthy idealization of one of the worst evils of our social life".[2] As a matter of fact, there is nothing extraordinary in Dumas's heroine or her action.

Not only idealistic reformers but also determined realists like Honoré de Balzac were swept off their feet by the new godly figure. "The moral of this", wrote Balzac in conclusion of *The Married Life of Fair Imperia*, in which the courtesan commits suicide for her lover's sake; "is that virtue is only known to those who have practised love." So the whore with the heart of gold was born, ever ready to sacrifice her life and comfort for those who need her. She exists in Tolstoy's Maslova, in Dostoevsky's Sonya, in Dickens's Nancy, in Brecht's Shen Te and in Sartre's Lizzie. Momentary glitters of the golden heart peep through the works of even those writers who had little knowledge of the underworld or occasion to study it. The dignified John Galsworthy gave us such a moment in *The Forsyte Saga*. In her despair, Irene goes to the river to commit suicide, but she is seen by a prostitute who hurries to her, pursuades her against it and takes her home. There, Irene is nursed by the prostitute for three days and put on the road back to a life of philosophic acceptance. The idolization of the whore is again coupled with the call of reform. In gratitude and in memory, Irene sets up a home for the rehabilitation of prostitutes.

The complete recipe for the romanticized version of the whore, from the hour of her fall, through her grisly career and into the dawn of redemption by the force of her corrosion-proof golden heart, is given in *Crime and Punishment*. Dostoevsky published this masterpiece in 1866, soon after the end of his Siberian imprisonment, when the Utopian socialist ideas of the Petrashevski group to which he belonged were still in his mind. *Crime and Punishment* represented Dostoevsky's transitional period before his complete conversion to an arch-reactionary writer. The novel was written after the emancipation of the serfs and the invasion of Russia's towns and cities by thousands of unemployed people with little to occupy them other than crime for the men and whoredom for the women. Dostoevsky drew a vivid picture of the squalid side of St Petersburg, which he knew like the back of his own hand, as well as Charles

Dickens knew the slummy streets of London. The Russian novelist starts by depicting the depressing background against which his heroine grew up, with the family brought to the point of starvation by her alcoholic father. Sonya goes up to her stepmother, Katerina Ivanovna, and tells her of a certain procuress who is urging her into the business. "Why not?" shouts the consumptive Katerina. "What is there to preserve so carefully?" The girl goes out and after two hours returns to give us this guilt-ridden piece of Dostoevsky's Christian mind:

> She came in and went straight to Katerina Ivanovna and laid thirty silver roubles on the table in front of her without a word. She looked at her, but she did not utter a single word, only took our big green woollen shawl – we have one which serves for all of us – wrapped it round her head and face and lay down on the bed, with her face to the wall, and her little shoulders and her whole body were trembling ... then I saw Katerina Ivanovna, also without a word, go to my little Sonya's bedside, and she stayed here on her knees all the evening, kissing her feet, and she would not get up, and then they both fell asleep with their arms round one another.

This romantic picture recurs in other places. As the drunkard father gets run over by a carriage and falls dying, he finds himself in the arms of his loving daughter. Dostoevsky, usually a master of psychology, is hindered here by this over-idealized picture of the harlot from applying any psychological logic to the noble Sonya. Her street-walking does not even scratch the surface of the religious Sonya, the loving, the tender, the well-mannered and the dedicated. She gives all the money she earns to her father and stepmother; she reads the New Testament to her beloved Raskolnikov; she finally persuades him to accept his punishment and seek a new life; she follows him to Siberia, brings food to the other prisoners and writes their letters for them.

> She would smile and bow to them; they were pleased when she smiled at them. They liked even the way she walked, turning round to watch her, and praising her; they praised her even for being so small; they could not find words to say in her praise. They even went to her when they were ill.

Sonya starts her career with that melodramatic scene of the weeping mother kneeling at the feet of the ravished girl, and ends it with another melodramatic scene with her lover, redeemed by her dedication, kneeling at her feet and clasping her knees; weeping by the bank of a river in the early morning.

The Woman with the Heart of Gold

An interesting aside comes from the writer in the episode of her brief incrimination. Luzhin, a lawyer endowed with all the wickedness, hypocrisy, greed and philistine ambitions of his class, involves Sonya in a theft staged by him. Like Tolstoy's Maslova, the whore is exposed to arrest for crimes which she did not commit, a common occurrence in police records.[3] Luzhin's frame-up, however, is frustrated by his companion, the communist Lebezyatnikov, who unmasks the lawyer's villainy. In the encounter between the two, Luzhin dismisses prostitutes as fallen women, born in wickedness and given to theft and all the antisocial habits associated with their profession. His idealist friend challenges that and puts the current communist view on the matter as understood by Dostoevsky:

> "In my opinion, that is, according to my personal conviction, it [prostitution] is the most normal condition for a woman. Why not? I mean we must make certain *distinctions*. In our present society, it is not, of course, entirely normal, because it is forced on her, but in future it will be completely normal, because freely chosen. And even now she had the right to act as she did; she was suffering, and that was her stock so to speak, her capital which she had a perfect right to dispose of. Of course, in the future society there will be no need of capital funds, but her role will be given a different significance, under harmonious and rational conditions. As for Sonya Semenovna, herself, in present condition, I look upon her action as a spirited concrete protest against the organization of society and I deeply respect her for it; I rejoice to see her."

Sonya appears in the incorruptible character of Tolstoy's Maslova in *Resurrection* (1899); the sixth illegitimate child of a milkmaid who produced babies one after the other, all properly and quickly baptized and then left to starve and die. The sixth baby did not die, but the mother did instead, and Maslova was brought up as an orphan. At the age of eighteen, she is seduced by Nekhlyudov, a nephew of her guardians, who happens to stay in the house on his way to his regiment. Maslova takes the road taken before her by nearly two-thirds of the Russian harlots, who were chambermaids made pregnant, kicked out into the streets, moved from one job to another and finally ended up in the brothels. All this is given in retrospect, for the great Russian novelist starts his story much later, with Maslova in the dock falsely accused of poisoning a merchant. On the jury sits none other than her first seducer, now an influential prince just considering marriage with a rich aristocratic lady. His recognition of the girl in front of him releases the whole mechanism of guilt.

When Maslova decided to choose her profession, she considered everything rationally and found prostitution the best possible work open to her. One of the elements which she took into account was the revenge which this career could give her on her seducer and his class. What the bourgeoisie wanted to avoid now came full circle to torment their inner conscience. The bourgeois recipe of reform and rehabilitation presents itself immediately to the prince, and his long crusade to save his victim begins. Maslova continues to be the good angelic girl who harbours no grudge, and in no time responds to his guidance by giving up smoking, drinking and coquetry. She does everything asked of her and becomes the idol of the prisoners. In Siberia, she begins to feel the new wind of revolution and finds her ideal in a revolutionary woman inmate.

A peculiar piece of psychology comes from the novelist. Both the revolutionary woman Mary Pavlovna and the prostitute Maslova Mikhaylovna share the dislike of sexual love. Yet love has not died in the heart of Maslova, as she soon meets her true one in the person of Vladimir Simonson, another marxist revolutionary. In the stock scene of the woman caught between two suitors, the prostitute recognizes that the love of the prince is motivated by his need for redemption, whereas the love of the revolutionary is the love of a free heart and clear conscience.

Had the story been Maslova's, the novel could have ended there, but Tolstoy was more preoccupied with himself as portrayed in Prince Nekhlyudov. *Resurrection* was based on a true story related to the writer, which brought to his mind another true story, this one about himself. In his adolescence, he also violated a young maid and made her leave the house pregnant. The novel focuses on the endeavour of the guilty man to redeem himself, during which the wronged prostitute manages to find her own salvation in the love of the one who understands her, leaving the wrongdoer high and dry. Tolstoy is therefore forced to add another, anticlimactic chapter, in which the prince finally finds his resurrection when he reads a passage from the New Testament. Chekhov's comment on the ending is fairly apt: "To throw it all away on a piece of scripture is a little too theological."[4]

Like Emile Zola and a whole line of committed writers, Tolstoy turned all his fury on the evils of society in his story of the prostitute. *Resurrection* is not one of his masterpieces, but it contains his strongest attack on the establishment in nearly all its branches – army, police, courts, prisons, the medical profession and the administration. In this merciless broadside, artistic construction and elegance of style are sacrificed. The naturalistic picture is distorted to allow for didacticism, the dimension of depth being increased to accommodate Tolstoy's perception of the evil that pervaded tsarist Russia.

Tolstoy took considerable pains in studying the milieu of *Resurrection*, and relied on extensive documentation. He described the sordid life of brothel-land, the sleepless nights of the whores and the humiliation of police check-ups. The mockery of law and justice which sends Maslova to Siberia through a technical error receives a venomous indictment charged with satire. When counsel for the defence refers to the hapless position of women subjected to the wicked exploitation of men, the President of the Court, who happens to hear this case on a day in which he has a rendezvous with a mistress, interrupts to rule this point out of order. The public prosecutor, on the other hand, repeats the prevailing doctrines on the heredity of sin and vice: the accused is not only a prostitute but the bastard daughter of a prostitute who tempted innocent men and engineered their ruin. The medical profession is implicated in the person of the prison practitioner with the "pimpled face" who denounces Maslova for refusing to humour his sexual advances. The perversion of religion is exhibited in an ingenious passage in which Nekhlyudov ravishes Maslova after attending a church service – carefully depicted by the writer – which has brought the emotions of the two young people to a pitch of exaltation and love.

The minions of officialdom, the police, judges and inspectors are reduced to malignant pests and ugly weeds. In the name of the government, they think that they can deal with people with indifference, for the government and not themselves will be the target of the blame. They imagine they can treat people without affection, as they treat bricks and trees. Yet, "people are like bees". You cannot make the most of them without care and affection. You must love them if you want anything from them, and if you do not, then don't ask them to do things for you. Stay in your place, Tolstoy goes on preaching, and occupy yourself with inanimate objects, or with your own self.

Resurrection is the novel nearest to revolutionary literature written by Tolstoy. For the first time, proletarian characters fill one of his stories in contrast to the peasant characters of his earlier works. It is also in this novel that we find the great humanist dealing in a positive manner with the ideas, ethics and aspirations of the Russian revolutionaries. For all this, and for its loaded attack on the evils of the tsarist régime, George Lukacs, the eminent Hungarian marxist critic, said that there was no single novel in all European literature that could match *Resurrection* in its epic greatness.[5] For the very same reasons the novel fell prey to censorship, and Tolstoy had to modify or delete many passages to meet the wishes of the censor before he could have it published. The bourgeois critics and moralists of many countries also did their best to attack this so-called piece of immoral literature.

Although the idealized type of prostitute, the fallen woman with the heart of gold, is not a rarity in actual life – the ease with which she is in fact repeatedly exposed to exploitation does not square with the alternative stereotype of her as being invariably self-seeking – militant revolutionaries totally rejected this romantic version. The hard prostitutes of Bertolt Brecht are more like the vigilant proletarians who are not easily taken in. They believe neither in the virtue of sentimental sacrifice nor in a religious or respectable salvation. Yet the pull of the romantic prostitute could not be resisted by Brecht himself, whose conversion to communism was soon celebrated in the visionary resurrection, à la Marx, of *The Good Woman of Setzuan.*

The image of the golden-hearted harlot in the underworld of a Western capitalist metropolis was not one that the German dramatist could accept. He must at least shift his stage to a land less gruesome. This was a period in which Brecht turned to the East for the source of his inspiration, but East or West the evil of society was there. Having lost all patience with humanity, and having decided to destroy this world, the gods agree to leave it alone if they can only find one good person still living in it. They descend on the Chinese town of Setzuan to search, but on their first night on earth they can find no one ready to give them accommodation except Shen Te, the prostitute, who even sends away her customers to make room for them. With the little money given to her by the gods, she hastens to seek her salvation and change her life by opening a tobacco shop. She distributes rice to the poor daily and opens her shop to the homeless and workless. Shen Te even buys water from the water-carrier on a rainy day. As in Bunuel's *Viridiana*, the demoralization of society has penetrated so deep, Shen Te discovers. that charity and kindness can achieve nothing but additional ruin. The poor have become like lepers who contaminate anyone who comes innocently to their rescue.

Everybody abuses Shen Te's good nature. Even the water-carrier sells her water in cups with false bottoms. The policeman objects to her former prostitution and suggests she marries one who was ready to sleep with her in holy matrimony for the money she would give him. As it happens, Shen Te encounters a man who is about to commit suicide after failing to achieve his ambition of flying. She saves him from death, restores his hope by giving him money with which to become a pilot, and finally falls in love with him. But he too wants to exploit her and take her money without her love.

Although Brecht's idealized whore is another variation of the woman with the heart of gold, he nevertheless does not allow her to meet the tragic end of Dumas's Camille or the mystic salvation of Dostoevsky's Sonya. Shen Te borrow's Brecht's microscope, puts the people of Setzuan under the lens, and prescribes a marxist remedy: work. She converts her charity shop to a tobacco factory in which her paupers can make a decent living, but only with honest and hard work. She smashes her sweetheart's romantic dreams of flying and makes him a shop steward in the factory. All the while, her pregnancy takes its course, promising the birth of a new life out of an act of genuine love, the love of a prostitute, and into a world of plenty in which all work according to their ability and each receives according to his or her needs.

Shen Te is only able to achieve this position by putting her golden heart aside, if only for a while, and then replacing it with a heart of steel. She has to split up her personality between Shen Te, "the girl who likes to please everyone, who lived and let live", and Shui Ta, her *alter ego*, disguised as her ruthless businesslike cousin. When she is in a romantic mood, she wears Shen Te's clothes and becomes the weak woman follishly kind and self-giving: "I would go with the man I love, I would not reckon what it costs me." When there is a business crisis, she wears Shui Ta's trousers and resumes the uncompromising role of her imaginary cousin. The old theatrical trick of Shakespeare's Rosalind and her successors is played out here with a loaded message. In a world of bestiality, you have to become a centaur – half human, half beast. In this respect, *The Good Woman of Setzuan* may be taken as a prologue to Brecht's often criticized position in East Germany and his philosophic approach to what he must have disliked there.

The Good Woman of Setzuan dramatized the "good/bad" vision which pervades Brecht's epic theatre. His dramatic theory, which rejected the theatrical illusion of reality with its professed naturalism and character psychology, ended in the didactic play in which the various characters became mouthpieces of black or white, good or evil. Where the two qualities of goodness and badness had to coexist in one character, as in the prostitute, the person was split into the two different components. This binary ethic became the butt of repeated criticism by those who did not accept the concept of didactic theatre.[6]

The generous nature of some women ever-disposed to please, as depicted in this literature and represented in pornographic terms in the American story *Candy*, by Terry Southern, is supported by the actual reality of everyday life: it is part of the psychology of at least one category of prostitutes whose self-giving nature is often the original cause of their drift towards brotheldom in a society that allows no place for goodness. In this society of exchange value, the bourgeois critic could only understand the whore's generosity as a manifestation of her psychopathy and the easy virtue of the fallen woman as a sign of an evil promiscuity which has nothing to do with men. (This was the conventional interpretation of Nana's squandering on Fontan and sleeping with young Georges.) The whore's generous nature is also expressed by Maxim Gorky in his play *The Lower Depths*, in the character of Nastia, the young streetwalker, who goes out to earn a few roubles and gives them to a good-for-nothing count who repays her by even making her do his house cleaning.

An attempt to create a more balanced picture of the good prostitute was Jean-Paul Sartre's *The Respectable Prostitute*, the play written after his visit to the United States and expressing his disgust with the American way of life. The position of the coloured people stood for him as a living indictment which allowed for no excuse. To cut still deeper, he took a prostitute for his heroine. The prostitute, Lizzie, receives an unexpected visit from a black man who implores her to tell the truth to the court in a murder case in which he has been falsely accused. The true white American soon arrives in the person of Fred, who makes love to the whore, pays her and offers her money to testify against the black man and cover up the real white murderer. When Lizzie scorns the money, and stands up to pressure and threats, the crafty politician in the person of Senator Clarke runs through a Boule de Suif routine, harping on patriotism and her own sense of responsibility towards the white community. The will of the noble prostitute is then broken, and Lizzie, however implausibly, looks forward to Fred's love and his family's respect. The better side of the whore wins in the end and comes to the rescue of the black man and her own good self when she discovers the depth of the respect of her white community for a woman like her.

Although filmed and staged in most countries, *The Respectable Prostitute* remains one of Sartre's weaker plays. His attempt at the portrayal of a three-dimensional character did not prove more effective than the flat take-it-or-leave-it representation of the noble prostitute. The whore is the quintessence of man's good and evil deeds in their starkest forms. Black and white may be the only pigments with which her story can be told.

The ambiguous attitude to the prostitute displayed by writers was extended to include her offspring too, as well as the offspring of any unmarried mother. The illegitimate child was held in abhorrence by all societies with a high regard for property, and the word "bastard" came to stand in many languages for the worst enemy of society. This notion was in turn translated into the reality of the great works of literature, as in Shakespeare's Edmund, the bastard son of Gloucester in *King Lear*. Opposition to the illegitimate child has obvious reasons which require little elucidation. In the age of reason, the old mystic fear was given the verisimilitude of science. Cesar Lombroso produced statistics which claimed that 65 per cent of the minors arrested in 1864 in France were bastards or orphans, and that 30 per cent of prostitutes in Hamburg, Germany, and recidivists in Italy were also illegitimate; he concluded that they became so "largely on hereditary influences".[7] This was quite mild in comparison to some if the weird theories elaborated by other sociologists. Promiscuity, immorality, criminality and prostitution were looked upon by such people as part of one's inborn fate. Such ideas impressed many novelists, including Emile Zola, who made this concept the driving force of his Rougon-Macquart series. Even *Nana*, which was meant to chastise society, reflected that influence, as Nana herself was the daughter of a dissipated woman, and Zola referred to her immorality as something "in her blood".

Opposite to this standpoint was the other attitude which idealized the illegitimate child beyond all recognition, even on the part of writers who were generally associated with naturalism and realism. The classic figure here is undoubtedly Dickens's Oliver Twist, whose sentimental goodness can hardly be matched by any other character in fiction or drama. Tolstoy's Pierre Bezukhov (*War and Peace*), who is invested with the sublime opinions and ideals of the writer, is another glorified example. In addition to her prostitute's career, illegitimacy was the second element which gave the presumption of goodness in Tolstoy's other noble person, Maslova. The bourgeoisie were caught in a dilemma: whether to undermine their property system by accepting the offspring of "fallen women", or to reject the increasing number of illegitimate children and face the social and financial burdens incumbent on that. The reformers and idealists opted for the more humane solution.

The early black writers of the assimilationist school fell under the spell of the same literary attitude to heredity and selected their good characters from the unlawful offspring of some erring white and a black partner, with the naive implication that white was a guarantee of a higher quality. The pretty mulatto girl, the fruit of white fornication, became the heroine who called for the admiration, love and pity of the reader of Negro literature before the age of revolt.[8]

The question of illegitimacy did not greatly engage the attention of socialist writers, as we may notice in *Mrs Warren's Profession*, for example. Although Vivie is a bastard, the question of her inheriting an inclination of vice from her mother and aunt does not arise, nor does the question of suffering degradation or rejection. Sir George Crofts, Mr Praed and the Reverend Samuel Gardner, all respectable representatives of the establishment and the church, are after her. Shaw even pokes fun at the idea of blood relationship by throwing in the possibility that any of them might actually be her father. The socialists who concerned themselves with the idea of heredity took a different leaf from natural history, namely Darwin's natural selection, in which both Shaw and William Morris found their guiding light in their treatment of social issues. Indeed, Morris went further in his attitude towards the bastard and gave the Oliver Twists fathered by the idealist school a scientific justification. In *News from Nowhere* (1891) he claimed that beauty and health had improved as a result of the new freedom felt in love. A child born out of a natural selection based on love, even if transient, was likely to turn out better than that of a respectable commercial marriage, he wrote.[9] Such was the sentiment felt by Charles Dickens about half a century before, when he started serializing *Oliver Twist* in *Bentley's Miscellany*. Oliver, the child conceived and born on the wrong side of the law but out of dear love and mutual attraction, grows up to be the handsome good-natured boy, while his legitimate half-brother Monks, born within a commercially arranged marriage, grows up to be an ugly man and wicked criminal, loathed by the author.

A different kind of revolutionary mystic fantasy about the character of the illegitimate son of a prostitute found a channel in Gorky's short story "Nilushka" about the down-and-outs of Russia. The scene is set this time in the poor suburb of Beuv, teeming with lawlessness, disease and newly freed serfs, where the only sounds to be heard are either of weeping or mad cursing, and the only singing is that of the bawd Felitzata. The majority of the women become pregnant with every winter, and on the arrival of the spring may be seen walking abroad with blue hollows under their eyes and with large stomachs. Everybody lives like lethargic animals stricken with sickness.

> Indeed, it is only the women of the place who, turbulently quarrelsome and hysterically noisy, spend most of the day in souring the streets with skirts tucked up, and never cease begging

The Woman with the Heart of Gold

for pinches of salt or flour, or spoonfuls of oil as they rail and screech at and beat their children, and thrust withered breasts into their babies' mouths, endeavouring to right their woebegone condition. Yes, all are dishevelled and dirty and have wizened, bony faces, and the restless eyes of thieves.

After this piece of socialist realism, Gorky goes on to give the same marxist interpretation of a harlot's life. "You see," says Felitzata in answer to the criticism of her conduct:

"I have had very much to bear, for there was a time when such hunger used to gnaw at my belly as you would never believe. It was then that my eyes became dazzled with the tokens of shame, so I took my fill of love, as does every woman, and once a woman has become a light-o-love, she may as well doff her shift altogether and use the body which God has given her. And, after all, an independent life is the best life; so I hawk myself about like a pot of beer, and say, 'Drink of this, anyone who likes, while it still contains liquor.'"

Against this typical background the author introduces Nilushka, the bastard son of Felitzata, the God's harlot of Beuv, to grow up and become the God's fool of the locality. Maxim Gorky's short story of "Nilushka" is full of spiritual colours and Christian imagery. The decadence, strife and misery of the town are reminiscent of the decline of Judea. Felitzata is very much a slavonic Mary in her nobility, courage, honesty and serene acceptance. Only her honest humility prevents her from attributing her son to God, but she is content to say that perhaps his father was a monk; for the son has a lot to recommend him as the awaited Messiah. He looks "like a thing which the earth has begotten of love. Yes, Nilushka was like an angel in some sacred picture adorning the southern or the northern gates of an ancient church." He walks on tiptoe, smiling and waving his arms in a manner which causes the ample folds of his sleeves and smock to flutter until he seems to be moving in the midst of a nimbus. The people love him and sneer at him, worship him and torment him, but no one can understand what he is saying. The landlord tries in vain to teach him what to say to the people, but he insists on singing instead. In the prime of his youth he dies with everything around him looking red: "he had been wounded, and was bleeding to death".

To socialists, the blood relationship of the child, whether legitimate or illegitimate, was immaterial. What mattered was the education and upbringing. Brecht emphasized the point in the moral of his play *The Caucasion Chalk Circle*, inspired by an anonymous Chinese play of that name dating back to the fourteenth century. The contest over the parenthood of a child is resolved by the judge by drawing a chalk circle around the child and asking the two claimant mothers to try to pull him out, each in her direction. The one who can bear to use force, and who succeeds in pulling him hard towards her, is not his mother, says the judge, as she was not mindful of hurting him, even if she was actually his real mother:

> That what there is shall go to those who are good for it,
> Thus, the children to the motherly, that they prosper,
> The carts to good drivers, that they are well driven,
> And the valley to the waterers, that it bring forth fruit.

8

The Eternal Shadow of the Warrior

A notable feature of prostitution is its epidemic increase at times of war, revolution and armed commotion, on account of the economic, social and psychological factors generated by such conditions of mortal conflicts. Wars invariably deprive young wives and lovers of their men folk, resulting in financial, sexual and emotional frustrations. At no time is the natural balance between the sexes more seriously disturbed than during wars, when thousands of men are thrown into one sector of the country and hundreds of towns and villages are left to women and children only. Loaded with booty, provisions and a fat salary, the warrior finds in the starving and displaced woman an easy target. To the enemy, she is just another prize of war to be ravished and subdued; to her compatriots, she must give all and humour the men who are dying for her king and country. The permanent threat of death and the cheapened price of life diminish the sanctity of human values and at the same time engender a burning desire to ensure the survival of human life by a crude response to the sex instinct. Interesting to note also how mass-murdering dictators have often urged their peoples to breed and breed, come what may.

The old relationship between sex and combat, known both to man and beast from times immemorial, acquired a new form and direction under the system of private property and its correlative trade in human beings and human labour, when brothels, brothel-keepers and their inmates became familiar parts of wars, including those fought in the name of religion. It was thus that Louis IX, the saintly king of France, issued an edict in 1254 ordering the exile of all prostitutes and bawds from his country, but when he went on to lead his army for the crusades, he was followed by a troop of harlots marching at the rear.[1]

This army formation was by no means extraordinary; it was quite customary for medieval armies to be escorted by what were known as camp followers. It was reported, for instance, that when the Duke of Alva invaded the Netherlands, his army was followed by 400 whores mounted on horseback and 800 on foot.[2] The naval fleets of the colonial powers adopted the procedure when anchored at ports of allowing prostitutes on board. There was even an occasion when the British Admiralty sent 200 whores to one of its ships when its men threatened to mutiny in demand for women.[3]

This phenomenon gathered more momentum during the last century when it became a world-wide problem affecting most colonial peoples, especially in India and Ireland. In the latter country, prostitutes lived just outside the bounds of the military camps, in nests of branches and bushes, often clothed with nothing but the flimsiest petticoats in anticipation of custom.[4]

In India, the British military authorities established procedures for recruiting, transporting and accommodating young prostitutes in specially designated quarters at government expense. The *mahaldarni* (brothel-keeper) used to be treated as a government employee on the lists of the hospital establishment. The deterioration in the conditions and health of the women and the associated risk of infection to Her Majesty's soldiers induced Whitehall to send a number of committees of enquiries to the Indian sub-continent. The Report on Prostitution and the Treatment of Venereal Diseases described the situation in these words:

> There is in effect a system of registration which, while it recognizes prostitution in general as an occupation permissible (like lawful trades) within the cantonment, does further afford to the prostitutes who attend the periodic examination a special recognition by the authorities which is unique both in its character and its object.[5]

A typical racial discrimination allowed European whores to live with the officers, whilst confining the much younger native girls, sometimes less than twelve years old, to the wretched conditions of the brothel. The Committee gave frightening details of the conditions which prompted the administration in 1898 to initiate a package of reforms.

In more recent history, cameramen and press reporters have made us quite familiar with the streets of shame and ignoble night clubs of Saigon under the US presence in Vietnam. The same may be said, albeit to a lesser degree, about Algiers during the war of liberation. One of the main centres for military fornication in the Middle East was Egypt, where the native government was compelled in 1935 to prepare a three-year plan to mitigate the problem. It seems, however, that the flare-up of World War II prompted the British military to inspire the Egyptian government to drop its attempt to curb prostitution and lend a hand to the war effort by allowing a series of new brothels to open in Alexandria and the Canal Zone. Hence, the number of registered prostitutes swelled in 1939 to 2,374 and the number of brothels rose to 831.[6]

The studies prepared by the League of Nations pointed to the existence of a relationship between the spread of venereal disease and the leave and pay-day of soldiers. One of its reports noted that the southern states of the USA had resorted to the importation of whores from Mexico for the sexual needs of the US Army.[7]

The social writers had no need for royal commissions of enquiry or League of Nations reports to bring to their attention this very recognizable situation. The clamour of war, thunder of guns, bursts of firearms and air-raid alarms filled, therefore, many of the stories and plays dealing with this subject against a backdrop of armed conflict and militarism. Indeed, many of the works already discussed in this book, from Wedekind's *Lulu* to Najib Mahfuz's trilogy, reflect the violence of arms associated with prostitution and give the message of protest a double edge against both war and whoredom.

In "Boule de Suif", Guy de Maupassant depicts the individual dignity and injury of the common whore in the wake of the national dishonour wreaked by the Germans in the 1870 war. As the occupation officer persists in demanding his right of conquest from the French female, the writer goes on to describe the harvest of the war, the humiliated gangs of defeated soldiers, the Avengers of the Defeat, the Citizens of the Tomb, the Companions in Death "looking like a horde of bandits", along their line of retreat.

In the Italian short story "Aminta", Giovanni Comisso relates how the two sinister forces of poverty and soldiery join hands in a two-pronged attack on the consumptive little girl of Siena, torn between her home, with an alcoholic father and a bereaved mother, and the army camp, with its teeming soldiers, beating the pretty streets of Siena with their heavy boots.

Najib Mahfuz's Egyptian heroine, Miriam, falls to a similar temptation as her country breaks under the weight of British occupation and bursts into war and revolution. The blind prostitute of the Iraqi poet Badr Shakir al-Sayyab also loses her virtue to soldiers from beyond the seas. In Jean Genet's play *The Balcony*, the action takes place to the accompaniment of gunfire, martial music and the outcries of killing and destruction as the play ends with a general revolution which sweeps away the complacent make-belief world of Irma's establishment.

Like Maupassant, Emile Zola selected the Franco-German War of 1870 as an appropriate setting for terminating Nana's life and career. During that frightful night in which the glorious whore expires, Emperor Napoleon III declares war on Germany. As her sickened body and horrific mask of a face lie decaying on her deathbed, the chanting of the patriotic demonstrator is heard outside repeating, "To Berlin! To Berlin! To Berlin!" Recoiling from her corpse, yesterday's admirer Fontan decides to enlist and join the war, while the other prostitutes sit around the heap of rotting flesh and discuss the war and the need to defend the honour of France and the Empire. It is significant to note the considerable condensation of time contrived by the author to link up the end of the harlot's progress with the outbreak of war and the eventual defeat of Napoleon III. It has been computed that, according to her life story and family history, Nana must have died at the age of eighteen, which, given the time sequence of events, was arithmetically impossible.[8] In this, the author was defying the element of time to synchronize the two factors of whoredom and war and turn the whole collection of the Rougon-Macquart novels into a monumental indictment of the society of the Second Empire with its greed, decadence and ruthless exploitation.

Alexander Kuprin established his literary reputation early in his life by publishing *The Duel*, in which the central theme was an attack on militarism. His next major work, *Yama* (translated as *The Pit*), linked up the non-violent sentiment with the theme of prostitution. The novel progresses from the goings-on of the sprightly wives of the soldiery and the plump widows secretly trading with vodka and free love at open brothels licensed by the authorities and mainly frequented by army cadets and soldiers, who boasting of having contracted VD, and ends up with the drunken men of arms demolishing the house and cursing the city.

A widely known and repeatedly quoted and misquoted story is Arthur Schnitzler's "Change of Partners", an amusing little work of 1900, in which the Austrian social reformed gave his frequent anti-bourgeois attacks a satirical turn by following the cycle of vice in his contemporary society. We first have the street-walker giving VD to the soldier, who gives it to the parlour maid, who gives it to the young man in the house, who gives it to the newly married wife. She in turn gives it to her husband, who gives it to his girl friend, who gives it to the poet. The poet infects the actress, who then gives it to the aristocrat, who takes it back to the street-walker and the cycle continues *ad infinitum*.

With its horrors and terrible waste of human life, the Great War inspired revolt and revulsion against wars in general in the hearts and minds of many writers, artists and political thinkers, who could no longer keep aloof in view of the newly introduced system of compulsory service. Some of them resisted the task by becoming conscientious objectors. Others who found themselves in the trenches wrote poems, songs and stories denouncing armed warfare and exposing the conditions at the war front. Quite a few left only their names in the history books of modern art and literature, while the rest returned alive to receive a further shock from the post-war deprivation of Europe. One way or another, this anti-militarist sentiment was magnified, especially in Germany, by its reflection in the looking-glass of the prostitute. The artists of German expressionism and Neue Sachlichkeit produced a long list of works projecting anti-militarist subject matter in terms of the degradation of feminism. War is the work of man; women are the victims of his work, and the opposition between the two often looks like a duel between death and life. As much as Brecht was obsessed with the prostitute as the obvious indictment of society, so was Otto Dix obsessed in his paintings with the street-walker of war-torn Europe as an indictment of militarism and all its ugly offsprings.

In the Anglo-Saxon world, we have two diverse examples in Sean O'Casey's play *The Plough and the Stars* and Joseph Heller's novel *Catch 22*.

Having received his education from the slums of Dublin, as he said, under the impact of the Great War and Irish rebellion, Sean O'Casey went on to write for the theatre in the vernacular language of its working class. In 1926, he came out with the tragedy *The Plough and the Stars*, in which he portrayed the long suffering of Ireland aggravated by violent chauvinism. In the land of its author, the play was booed and harassed, and the performance was turned into a mob demonstration against the playwright and the theatre company.

O'Casey places the action in the midst of the Great War and times Acts III and IV to coincide with the bloody Easter 1916 uprising of Dublin. As the play develops, the author introduces Rosie, a regular pick-up whore of one of Dublin's sleazy pubs. Through its windows is heard the noise of army units marching towards the Western Front to the tune of "It's a long way to Tipperary", while the military band plays martial music. Jingoistic speakers address the recruits in a public meeting, urging the people to enlist and fight for God, king and country. Rosie sits down dejected in this hopeless day of hers:

Th' solemn lookin' dials on th' whole o' them an' they marchin' to th' meetin'. You'd think they were th' glorious company of th' saints, an' th' noble army of martyrs thrampin' through th' streets of paradise. They're all thinkin' of higher things than a girl's garthers.

In a telling scene in which the whore tries to catch a customer and talks of the hardships of her life, especially on a patriotic day like this, the silhouette of the speechifying orator is projected behind the window:

It is a glorious thing to see arms in the hands of Irishmen .... We must accustom ourselves to arms and their use. We must not be afraid of bloodshed. A nation afraid of bloodshed loses its manhood. There are many things worse than bloodshed and slavery is one of them.

The irony of it is that the orator is speaking on behalf of England and the British Empire, but the words would sound just the same for Rosie were they said in a Republican meeting against the English. She finds no reason for dissent and agrees that it is important to fight for the country's freedom. Her intervention leads her into a discussion with the marxist Covey. Freedom, he tells her, is meaningless without economic freedom, and Rosie agrees here again: "They're not goin' to get Rosie Redmond to fight for freedom that wouldn't be worth winnin' in a raffle." Covey urges her to read Comrade Jenersky's *Thesis on the Origin, Development and Consolidation of the Evolutionary Idea of the Proletariat*. Rosie reminds him, however, that a pair of transparent silk stockings on the legs of a young girl in his lap would be a better proposition, and the professional whore uncovers her bosom and chases the young revolutionary in a little comic scene, preceding the storm.

Carrying the banner of the revolution, the banner of the Plough and the Stars, three Irish Volunteers burst in and take the oath of dying for Ireland. The play ends in a commotion of gunfire, clamour, ambulance sirens and the tragic cries of women, as the city plunges into the Easter uprising, but not before Rosie Redmond manages to secure a customer and the two stagger out drunk into the dark night singing "Dancin' a jig in th' bed an' bawlin' for butter and bread".

World War II was satirized in another story involving the life of prostitutes, when Joseph Heller, little known till then, published in 1961 his memorable *Catch 22*, the anti-war novel which has been filmed, televised and plagiarized, and occupies in relation to World

War II the position occupied by Jaroslav Hasek's *The Good Soldier Schweik* for World War I.

In his caustic attack on militarism and the empty grandeur of generals, Heller uses the character and career of the prostitute to depict the feverish energy of officers in their pursuit of the two capitalist obsessions of accumulation of wealth and debasement of sex and love into a "multi ficky-fick all day long". "Do you remember the whore who went on hitting me on my head with her shoes when we were naked?" says one officer to another.

At an American air-base in the Mediterranean, a group of officers divide their time between launching orgies of devastation on Italian towns and holding sex orgies at their brothels. The triangle of this little capitalist jungle is completed with the addition of illegal trading in the name of free enterprise pursued by the energetic Milo, who commissions the destruction of his own air-base at cost price plus 6 per cent to be paid by the Germans. On the other hand, a prostitute has her hair shaved off for sleeping with a German.

Catch 22 gives long accounts of the brothel life, the sleepless nights of the tired whores, the antics of the drunken soldiers, etc. Unlike the hard Brechtian women, Heller's heroines are innocent females with golden hearts driven into the business by hunger and need for US dollars. Into this world flies Yossarian, the pilot of Assyrian origin, looking for a crude sexual diversion, but his inner humanity leads him to the romantic Luciana and the adventure throws him into a tortured affection.

Soon after, the scene shifts poignantly to the military hospital, the operation theatre, the bizarre casualties, the face of death, pain and deformity, the soldier in white, whose entire body is crushed and rebuilt in plaster. Exhausted mentally and physically, Yossarian goes back to his room to find a dead soldier who cannot be disposed of because he is simply unaccountable. Yossarian then sinks into a depressive mood, guilt, anxiety and fears of tumours and terrible diseases.

Whereas the whores and their clients sit and discuss war and peace and indulge in idiotic orgies, Milo expands his business as far as India and Liberia and captures the entire cotton market of Egypt. He criticizes his colleages for spending their time with prostitutes when there are goods waiting for their aircraft, now decorated with emblems of justice, honour, liberty and patriotism. Hearing of the confiscation of a German aeroplane smuggling goods from the occupied zone, he bursts out in disgust. What is this? Is this Russia? When has it become the policy of the US government to confiscate private property? The aircraft belongs to the syndicate and everyone has a share in it. Soon afterwards he turns the attention of the syndicate to the traffic in white slavery, and the US air force begins to shift women from one market to another.

The novel is a series of bizarre anecdotes and adventures analysing the whore-warrior relationship and the degeneration of humanity under the impact of war. Almost hysterical, Nately's whore tries to kill Yossarian whom she holds responsible for her lover's death. "Why the hell shouldn't she? It is a man's world, and she and everyone younger had every right to blame him and everyone older for every unnatural tragedy that befell them." All this desperate love for the shy and inhibited Nately goes back to the day when he allowed her to have eighteen hours of unbroken sleep. Nately, on the other hand, fell in love with her when he saw her bored and stripped, exposing herself to the men in uniform. This is the world of the faked and the real, the uniformed versus the naked. In one scene the drunken commanders take off their clothes and puzzle out whether there is really no German among them. In another scene, in which their clothes are thrown out into the street, they find themselves unable to prove their high military ranks.

Under the burden of guilt, Yossarian starts looking for Nately's whore and her twelve-year-old sister, and the search reveals for him the misery of the Eternal City and the bestiality wreaked upon its women by his comrades:

> What a lousy earth! ... How many people were destitute that same night ..., how many homes were shanties, how many husbands were drunk and wives socked, and how many children were bullied, abused or abandoned. How many families hungered for food they could not afford to buy? how many hearts were broken? How many suicides would take place that same night, how many people would go insane? How many cockroaches and landlords would triumph ...?

Yossarian goes on piling up the miseries, concluding: "When you added them all up and then subtracted, you might be left with only the children, and perhaps with Albert Einstein and an old violinist or sculptor somewhere."

Along his path, he comes across a band of drunken soldiers having it away with a drunken woman by the side of the Ministry of Public affairs. "Pleesh, don't," pleads the female. "Come on, baby. It's my turn now." The brief words mix with the evocative scrape of an iron shovel against the concrete pavement as someone shifts the snow. Yossarian's flesh crawls with horror. The tour eventually leads him to a crowd gathering around the corpse of the imbecile Michaela smashed on the pavement. "I only raped her once," remonstrates his colleague who threw the wretched girl from the window.

Yossarian quits in the end in a little boat, but the warrior's escape includes none of the inhabitants of brothel-land. In this, one almost senses a subconscious desire on the part of writers and artists to keep the prostitute alive as a limitless source of inspiration. As such, she is not only the eternal shadow of the warrior but also an indisposable device for authorship and creative work. All things said, we all seem to need her.

9

The Avenger and her Problem

The apparition of the prostitute haunted writers from the beginning of the nineteenth century – a development which calls for the attention of the critic, the sociologist and the historian. What made this problem so fascinating to so many men of letters? There were far more tragic aspects of society than the matter of selling and buying sex but, for whatever reason, people continued to treat the fall of a woman as something worse than death. Death, indeed, was accepted as God's work, for which people might disclaim responsibility, but prostitution was looked upon as the work of man. The whore as the quintessence of the existing society was a general conception common among thinkers of all shades of opinion. W. Leck, who represented the Christian version of social history, described the prostitute as "the perpetual symbol of the degradation and sinfulness of man".[1]

It is a widely held view that there is something wrong in the sexual or family life of the married man who goes to whores. In Chapter 2, we mentioned how an inhuman lifestyle, commercial marriage and repressive puritanism batten down the natural sexual inclinations and force them eventually to leap out in a demonic orgy of perversions and excesses. In Jean Genet's magical play *The Balcony*, we encounter the weird world of Irma's sex establishment, which the brothel-keeper calls "The House of Illusion", with all its sexual perversions and fantasies, and to which men run away from their mundane and depressing life to dress themselves up in the guise of bishops, great generals and supreme judges, or pretend to be mighty warriors mounting their horses. The writer was apparently obsessed with the play, which he wrote and rewrote in many versions, finally introducing into the last scene the event of a revolution which sweeps away this little world of illusions by introducing the outside realities of injustice, poverty and exploitation of society on the one hand and the new set of revolutionary delusions on the other.

Chantal, one of the girls of this establishment, runs away and joins the social convulsion under the slogan "The revolution begins by denouncing the make-believe", which may explain the description of *The Balcony* by Harold Hobson, the *Sunday Times* critic, as a trial of reality by fantasy.

The brothel becomes a therapeutic asylum, staffed by human dolls in which men can stick the pins and needles of their anger and frustration and allay the inhuman estrangement of their souls. During the nineteenth century, the child prostitute furnished the ideal therapeutic doll, and the infant schools, as they used to call these expensive vice houses in industrialized England, provided ideal whoring fantasies to the leaders of trade and industry and made its contribution to the building of the British Empire. Procurers had even to tap continental sources to satisfy the rising demand for virgins in London. "Our business is in maidenheads, not in maids," said one. "My friends take the girls to be seduced and take them back to their situations after they have been seduced, and that is an end to it as far as we are concerned."[2] This is only one of the least sinister aspects of the sadistic and masochistic sex orgies which were common practices in Europe's brothel-lands.

As poignantly remarked in Jean Genet's play, to enter a brothel meant the rejection of the real world, and the unconscious realization of this fact disturbed the mental peace of the participants – the masters and makers of the existing social reality. The moral and financial "hangover" which followed the orgies and sexual debasement actuated the mechanism of guilt, a process which characterized the bulk of the nineteenth-century literature dealing with the prostitute. It is not a coincidence in the least to find a harlot lurking in nearly all the major works of that great master of the guilt neurosis novel, Dostoevsky. Zola's approach to prostitutes also reflects his own painful family life.[3] Tolstoy started his adolescent years with the violation of a helpless maid in his house, an event which must have kept preying on his conscience until he finally resolved it by redeeming that girl, not in reality but in the dream world of a novel. Indeed, the guilt complex often expressed itself more definitely in such matters as the revulsion from flesh shown by Zola in *Pot-Bouille*, and his general identification of nudity with moral evil – the old biblical appreciation. In *Nana*, Count Muffat reveals an almost pathological fear of the flesh as he recalls to his father confessor the image of the half-naked maid whom he saw by chance during his childhood, an image which returned to him when he saw the nude figure of Nana on the stage. "She must be the devil incarnate," was his fatalistic remark. The same revulsion is exhibited by Tolstoy in *Resurrection* when the hero of the story feels a shudder against the naked flesh appearing in the painting of *his mother* dressed in a black frock that reveals the white skin of her shoulders and bust.

Yet the prostitute is not quite a rag doll in which to stick pins and needles. She has a soul of her own, and this unhappy discovery plagues the comfort of her seducer. Yesterday's child-whore and violated chambermaid returns to gnaw at the conscience of the guilty and corrode the economic and social foundation of society. The revenge of the whore became another theme which preoccupied writers. In *The Idiot*, Dostoevsky makes Natasya Filippovna, the poverty-stricken orphan seduced at the age of sixteen by her wealthy benefactor Totsky, the messenger of revenge. She installs herself in his St Petersburg flat, spreading havoc in his life and obstructing all his chances to get married and achieve a regular profitable middle-class life. The former prey in the strong arms of the man finally renders the man a helpless prey between her stronger white legs. Totsky tries to kill himself to escape, but in the end he offers to pay his way out by offering her in marriage to whoever is ready to take her together with 75,000 roubles. Natasya makes her suitors keep on asking for more, but she spurns Totsky's money in the end and walks out with a man she likes. The revenge of the fallen woman appears again in Dostoevsky's last novel, *The Brothers Karamazov*.

The great symbol of vengeance scourging the evil society of the bourgeoisie came from Emile Zola in that memorable whore of all times, Nana. Her story takes up from Zola's previous novel *L'Assommoir*, the proletarian tragedy in which Coupeau, the tinsmith, becomes an alcoholic after an industrial accident, and Gervaise the laundress, his wife, falls into sin and becomes alcoholic as well, after the disintegration of her husband. Nana, the daughter, grows up in this squalor and misery. No sooner does she mature than she is ravished by a rich button manufacturer. Irresistibly beautiful, she becomes the desire of all Paris and the ruin of many good men. Their destruction becomes almost her mission in life, so much so that when she meets a respectable man like Count Muffat she feels instantly perturbed and sets her seduction mechanism into motion.

Nana speaks with a real working-class accent and cannot even spell the simplest words. Yet the smell of animal in her maddens Muffat and draws him nearer and nearer to his doom. In her new country house she flirts with him while another representative of the bourgeoisie, the Jewish banker Steiner, waits upstairs and the young Georges hides behind the curtain. In another passage reminiscent of

Maupassant's Marquise Obardi (the "fallen woman" who is the mother of the heroine of his story "Yvette", Nana repeats a similar challenge to the "honest woman". After a verbal duel with Muffat, who warns her not to talk of honest women as she does not know them, Nana strips naked and faces him: "I don't know them! Why, they aren't even clean, your honest women aren't! They aren't even clean! I defy you to find me one who could dare show herself as I am doing. Oh! You make me laugh with your honest women!" To complete the comparison with Maupassant's Marquise Obardi, Nana reminds Muffat that his wife is at that moment in the arms of the insignificant Fauchery.

Muffat the pious, the rich aristocrat, the hypocrite who says his prayers and crosses himself before and after every act of intercourse with the whore, is destroyed, his wealth squandered, his virtuous wife seduced, his state honours trampled underfoot. Nana orders him to come in his full uniform as the Chamberlain of the Court. She makes him creep on all fours: "Oh, get along with ye, Chamberlain," and showers him with kicks. Zola goes beneath her skin: "Oh, those kicks! How heartily she rained them on the Tuileries and the majesty of the Imperial Court, throning on high above an abject and trembling people. That is what she thought of society! That was her revenge." The whore proceeds to make the Count trample under his boots all the medals and honours awarded to him. She orders him to become an animal and starts to whip him (which he incidentally enjoys). In his pain, the pious Count remembers the holy saints who used to eat their own shit.

Nana is not finished with her society. She turns to Foncarmont and wipes out his life savings in a fortnight. There is also the landed la Faloise, who lasts a little longer – six weeks. "At every mouthful Nana swallowed an acre." The press does not escape her either, as she soon takes over Fauchery's newspaper and collects its income. Philippe has to steal money for her and ends up in prison, whilst his brother Georges stabs himself, leaving a bloodstain which cannot be cleaned off the carpet. "Bah! That'll wear off underfoot," she observes. And there is still the banker, Steiner:

> All these savings, the pounds of the speculators and the pence of the poor, were swallowed up in the Avenue de Villiers. Again he was partner in an iron works in Alsace; where, in a small provincial town, workmen, blackened with coal dust and soaked with sweat, day and night strained their sinews and heard their bones crack to satisfy Nana's pleasures. Like a huge fire, she devoured all the fruits of stock-exchange swindling and the profits of labour. This time she did for Steiner. She brought him to the

ground, sucked him dry to the core, left him so cleaned out that he was unable to invent a new roguery.

Nana eventually dies of smallpox, contracted from her son. Had she died from pox and not smallpox, the story would have become a simple morality tale of retribution, and the whore would have been convicted of evil-doing by her creator. Smallpox is a disease, however, which could hit anybody, whore or otherwise. The thesis of Henriques that Zola's great masterpiece is a moral story of paying the penalty for whoredom does not account for the sequence of events in the novel, except perhaps in one sense. Nana contracts her fatal disease from her own child whom she has neglected, exactly as the body social is visited by destruction from the woman whom it has ill-treated. Zola seems to be still working here within the nineteenth-century bourgeois structure of no escape for the harlot. She may find redemption for her soul, but not her life, which is almost the opposite of what Bertolt Brecht managed to put on stage.

Of course, this point can only make sense if we really take Nana as a naturalistic human being, for Emile Zola, notwithstanding his professed scientific realism, was painting in her a post-impressionist picture in which the surface realities were ignored for the sake of the inner essence.[4] The prostitute became, once more, a symbol, a vampire of revenge, a messenger of revolt. Her creator needs no further help from the critic, for he himself wrote:

> The fly that had flown up from the ordure of the slums, bringing with it the ferments of social decay, had poisoned all these men by merely alighting on them. It was well done – it was just. She had avenged the beggars and the wastrels from whose cast she issued. And whilst, metaphorically speaking, her sex rose in a halo of glory and beamed over prostrate victims like a mounting sun shining brightly over a field of carnage, the actual woman remained as unconscious as a splendid animal, and in her ignorance of her task was the good-natured courtesan to the last.

Like most works which presented the prostitute as an indictment of society, *Nana* was persecuted by the establishment. In France, a lawyer applied for an injunction to stop Zola from using his name in the "obscene" novel. The publisher of the story in England was prosecuted, fined and imprisoned for publishing pornographic literature. The critics of the day, on the other hand, confused the message of the novel, and Zola's preoccupation with some speculative theories of heredity added to the confusion. The emphasis on the environment and social evils of the Second Empire which Zola made the backbone of *Nana* and *L'Assommoir*[5] was played down to allow a free hand for the psychologist. Nana was treated as a psychopath devoid of any natural and human logic reasonably related to her environment and its social organization, while the story of her life and her parents' lives was pushed to the background.

Zola had almost foreseen this. In the society of Count Muffat, Nana tries to give accounts, in her own vulgar style and proletarian accent, of her early life and the goings-on in the tenement in which she grew up. Muffat frets with discomfort and tries to stop her from unfolding her past. In another passage revealing Zola's purposes, the novelist makes the journalist Fauchery write of Nana the actress: "with her, the rottenness that was allowed to ferment among the people was rising back up to the aristocracy. She is becoming the force of nature, a power of destruction ... corrupting Paris between her snow-white thighs."

In *David Copperfield*, the fallen hairdresser, Miss Mowcher, bears Dickens's message of revengeful justice. As she is discovered to be the culprit in the ruin of Little Emily, she speaks of her own abuse by the men who treated her as a plaything and an object of amusement, to be thrown away as they tired of it. "I must live," she protests. "I do no harm. If there are people so unreflecting or so cruel as to make a jest of me, what is left for me to do but to make a jest of myself, them and everything? If I do so, for the time, whose fault is that? Mine?" Amidst her streaming tears, the unhappy woman goes on to describe, in a lengthy passage, the deprivation, contempt and indifference of the society around her to a woman of her kind. Miss Mowcher, in fact, has little bearing on the course of the story except to create this opportunity for a sermon by Dickens.

The idea of revenge intrigued many writers, including Bernard Shaw, who considered the venereal diseases as the harlot's means of revenge on the society which ruined her. The psychoanalysts focused their Oedipus lenses on her and came to the conclusion that the whore is an angry woman bent on tormenting society in an act of vendetta against her despotic parents.[6] The industrial society adopted an ambivalent attitude towards the whore, analogous to that of the Christian church. She is sometimes seen as a wicked creature and sometimes as an angel of mercy. Both aspects reflect the persistent need for her and horror of the result of this need. The two attitudes followed one after the other in Tolstoy, whose early indulgence himself in selfish sexual adventures was followed by a remorseful revulsion from sex and girls, a period in which he described all women except mothers as "prostitutes".[7] In his more mature years, all prostitutes became godly women and mothers.

Nana and the collection of sluts who inhabit Zola's world belong also to the destructive category of whores. On the other side, we find the good prostitutes who people the stories of Maupassant, Tolstoy and Dostoevsky. They make the romantic heroines of many plays and novels, and disturb the realism of a great portion of progressive literature. Neither Bertolt Brecht nor Jean-Paul Sartre could escape the temptation of the romanticized whore in *The Good Woman of Setzuan* and *The Respectable Prostitute*.

Interestingly enough, women are often harder on their "fallen" sisters than men, perhaps because whoredom is the most formidable competitor with wedlock. In *Nana*, the aristocratic ladies of the Countess Sabine clique are shocked when they hear of the Parisian gutter whore coming to live near them, and devise the best method of showing contempt to this untouchable creature by ignoring her.

The duality of attitude owes a great deal to the peculiar constitution of industrial society, and is no more than an extension of the numerous contradictions which exist in its folds. As pointed out before, the merchant could not live without his whore, and the most mercantile society of all must produce the greatest number of whores. The capitalists were quick to produce those ideologists who preached that prostitution was necessary. One scholar praised fornication as a safe means of controlling population growth.[8] Bernard de Mandeville called in his *Modest Defence of Public Stews* (1724) for the organization of prostitution. In France, Rétif de la Bretonne published *La Pornographe* (1770) in which he put detailed plans for the organization of prostitution in healthy palaces of pleasure. Jean-Jacques Rousseau followed his nature theories and claimed that some women were naturally made for prostitution.

The anthropology of the nineteenth century, led by Lombroso, dwelt on the physical characteristics of prostitutes which made harlotry their inescapable career. Mayhew, who studied London's down-and-outs, started his monumental work by emphasizing the physical differences between the wandering people, who included the beggars and whores, and the settled people, who recognized "the rights of property and reciprocal social duties ... thus acquiring wealth and forming themselves into a respectable caste".[9]

In the 1870s, Tolstoy also considered prostitution as unavoidable and necessary for the numerous bachelors who lived in the modern industrial cities, as well as for the husbands who wanted to find a diversion from their wives. "It would be impious and unintelligent to pretend", he wrote, "that God was wrong to tolerate this state of affairs and Christ had been wrong to pardon one of them."[10] Bernard Shaw too conceded the argument that the modern cities were producing a large army of bachelors who could not marry until their forties and who must be catered for sexually until then. Wives must be protected from the hungry wolves by the institute of prostitution – the breakwater of marriage as he called it. Indeed, the Russians called prostitution "the necessary social evil".

Yet it soon produced its dreadful side-effects. The spread of venereal disease reached crippling proportions; the rise in illegitimacy and disabled prostitutes (often at an age as early as thirty) put heavy burdens on the rates and social services; the increase in crime and vice required more prison warders and policemen on duty. The leaders of the new industrial society took a leaf from their freshly discovered economic law of diminished returns. They found out that they could not exploit the prostitute endlessly and unconditionally because there was a ceiling above which the attempt backfired and produced a diminished benefit. The over-exploited and ill-treated whore acquired that spirit of vengeance so lethal to the pillars of society. The problem of vice was also found detrimental to the new industries. One English cigar manufacturer, for example, protested against the increase in brothels and dancing shops because they made his female workers tired, increased absenteeism, and finally reduced the productivity of his factory. A clergyman complained that prostitution was creeping into domestic service,[11] forgetting, of course, that domestic service was responsible for the seduction of many innocent girls. In numerous parliamentary debates in Britain and elsewhere, the problem of prostitution, or what was called "the social evil", and its impact on the taxes and rates, was lamented.

The most ominous development for the ruling establishment was the spread of venereal disease among the soldiers and sailors. William Acton, the physiologist who made a careful study of prostitution in England, found that 50 per cent of all diseases hitting the public came from prostitutes, but the naval and military services were much the most exposed targets. He found that one in five of the troops in the United Kingdom, the Mediterranean and British America suffered from these diseases between 1830 and 1837.[12] Mayhew also gave the same ratio for the incidence of syphilis in the British army between 1837 and 1847.[13] The League of Nations report depicted an even darker picture of the Netherlands Indies Army in 1911.[14]

The adverse effect of this threat to the health of the guards and watchdogs of the overseas market was alarming to their employers. Dr Acton examined this aspect of the venereal scourge in the light of the statistics of the Dreadnought Hospital, and found that the syphilis patients were put on the lists of "non-effective" for twenty-one days and cost the Treasury a thousand pounds annually.[15] In the second half of the nineteenth century, the problem reached such frightening proportions in the British Indian army that special commissions of inquiry were sent to India and legislation was passed to deal with the problem. A series of studies was also published in the major European countries, among which we should mention the classic book on the subject, *Die Prostitution*, written by Iwan Bloch in Germany at the turn of the century. Henry Mayhew, notably in *London Labour and the London Poor* (1861), and William W. Sanger, in his *History of Prostitution* (1858), dealt with the problem as it existed in England.

William Acton was certainly the outstanding spokesman for the bourgeois position vis-à-vis the "master problem". In his book *Prostitution*, he reiterated the claim that some women were born harlots. Vanity, he found, was the main cause of prostitution, and idleness and vanity were inevitable bequests from parent to child. He went on to draw on his experiences as a medical practitioner in France, and asserted that the children of prostitutes consigned by the police to the Lazare Hospital of Paris almost invariably became prostitutes, "notwithstanding all the religious teachings of the Sisters of Charity".[16] Such ideas presented in the respectable jargon of science made a considerable impression on the creative writers of the period, who more often than not portrayed their fallen women as the seeds of fallen women. The harlots were thus designed to be harlots, and society should be pleased with that because men needed them for the purpose of extramarital sex. Acton also quoted figures to show that, in fact, the prostitutes were better off than other women of the working class. The question was, therefore, not how to wipe out the "social evil", but how to organize it. The role of the prostitute must be accepted, hygiene must be provided and regulations made. The "fallen women" called for special legislation and attention like "murderers, thieves, gamblers and other male members of the dangerous classes".[17]

The hub of nearly all the reform studies was how to keep the prostitute healthy and free from venereal disease so that the gentlemen of society might make the most of them with the least trouble and expense. This was the principle on which all anti-prostitute legislation was based. That the law was not interested in the morals or ethics of the question but with the outward conduct of the prostitute was an observation made by the Street Offences Committee: "We are concerned not with prostitution itself but with

The Avenger and her Problem

the manner in which the activities of prostitutes and those associated with them offend against public order and decency, expose the ordinary citizen to what is offensive or injurious ...."[18] For years, magistrates throughout Britain spent hours trying to establish this one essential point, whether or not the prostitute had caused *annoyance* while practising her work.

Acton's "vanity" was re-echoed in the works of many specialists in the question. Of the more recent assertions made in the literature of prostitution is that of Seymour-Smith, who believes that "some women like being prostitutes". They may not like making love, just as typists may not like typing, but they still go on typing:

> It is now time to put the profession on a proper footing .... By nationalizing prostitution, providing attractive pensions for whores, and giving them expert training, we should considerably improve the nation's economy. A brothel in the House of Commons would improve the quality of debate by releasing sexual tensions in the proper place. The pathologically shy, the crippled, the hopelessly perverse, would all be catered for. The prostitute, paid a decent salary, would have a place of honour in the community as a highly skilled worker.[19]

Although these bizarre suggestions may appear to be a *jeu d'esprit*, there is actually nothing extraordinary about them. Most civilizations which needed mass prostitution have produced their own systems, but the capitalist organization failed to follow suit. At first one is inclined to wonder whether it was Christianity that prevented such a development, but this is only fractionally true. The real cause may be found in the essence of the capitalist system, the jungle of *laissez faire*. Henriques affirms in his commendable work that with the rise of industrialism, the old municipally organized prostitution gave way, in fact, to individual enterprise.[20] Prostitution was, therefore, played by ear. Such remedies as the transportation of whores to the colonies, the punishment of the seducers, the education of the girls, the improvement of the dwellings of the poor, the strengthening of religion, the facilitation of marriage were suggested to the community, and all these ideas vibrated in the various schools of the literature of prostitution. But two images captured the imagination most powerfully. The first was the appalling poverty and living conditions of the masses, which made their women easy targets for the procurers; the second was the commercial marriage of the wealthy – taking a spouse for the maximum economic benefit – which made the men seek love and sexual excitement in the arms of any women other than their wives. According to the bulk of progressive writers, the blame was to be shifted from the brow of the whore; her face now shone with the light of a false but golden dawn. Enter the woman with the heart of gold, side by side with the woman with the sword of revenge, in the fiction and drama of modern times. This is now the time to turn to the romantic version of the whore.

10

Redemption

With the idea of convicting the prostitute came the idea of redeeming her. Prostitution is the one long-established profession which has a short duration – a score of years at best. What becomes of the prostitute is an old question whose answer became very urgent in modern times. The problem of what to do with the hordes of ageing and incapacitated brothel inhabitants was intensified by the addition of the child whores, the virgin girls in their early teens or even younger who were used only once for the act of deflowering and were then turned out. The pressure on the taxes for their maintainance touched the hearts of the middle class, and the question of reclamation emerged. Various societies were formed for that purpose, and many bored gentlemen and chaste old maids found the work they provided very rewarding and spiritually uplifting. The Society for Juvenile Prostitution was formed to deal with child whores and deflowered girls. A number of homes were opened for prostitutes of humble origins, and other dignified homes for those who came from respectable families. The Magdalen Hospital, which belonged to the first category, admitted some 2,476 repentant whores in 1786 alone.[1] Many intellectuals who dealt in their writing with the problem of prostitution and the character of the whore concerned themselves with the work of reform in this field or participated in the organization of such homes.

Yet reclaiming the fallen woman proved to be an intractable problem. The prostitutes did not want to go to these homes and the community did not want to accept the repentant whores. In 1816, out of 130 prostitutes who were admitted to the institution of Bridewell, only twenty-one women accepted the offer of rehabilitation and only fifteen of these availed themselves of the offer of assistance.[2] The reason is obvious enough: prostitutes did not join the vice business blindfolded, as the do-gooders wanted to imagine. The notion of the prostitute as the innocent simpleton seduced by wicked men, as often staged in the popular melodramas of the nineteenth century, distorted the vision of such people and swept aside the pragmatic rationale of women like Shaw's Mrs Warren.

Shaw's marxist analysis was not, of course, a palatable one to the middle class; they preferred to believe more in the inherent element of venality existing in the bosom of every prostitute. Dr Acton summed up the notions common among his contemporaries in three principles: first, once a harlot, always a harlot; secondly, there is no chance for the moral or physical improvement of the prostitute; thirdly, the progress to decline of the prostitute is a short and rapid one.[3] According to Henriques's accounts, all the nineteenth-century societies for the reform of prostitutes reported that the community at large had not accepted the repentant prostitute in its midst. The irrevocable offence with its irrevocable banishment became the theme which consumed so much ink and so much midnight oil. Nearly every writer who portrayed the prostitute or referred to her situation had to halt here and pronounce an opinion.

Nevertheless, the redemption of the female sinner was not an altogether new development in literature. One of the earliest pieces on the subject was Thomas Dekker's *The Honest Whore*, printed in 1604. In this Jacobean play, the whore, Bellafront, tries to seduce Hippolito, who admonishes her and reminds her of her lewdness. His words arouse in her a feeling of shame, and so begins her great effort to redeem her life. She eventually repents and gets married. A series of calculated attempts to test her prove only her true and unshakeable fidelity, which makes her father and the court accept her.

That the idea of the whore's redemption should have obsessed the Western mind more than elsewhere is to some extent due to the Christian tradition behind it. The story of Mary Magdalene and her forgiveness by Christ went on inspiring religiously-minded thinkers and reformers. Indeed, one of the earliest institutions for the reform of the prostitute was opened by Theodora, wife of the Emperor Justinian. After a long life of dissolution and sexual vulgarity as a prostitute, she was converted to Christianity, repented her past life, and opened a home for her kindred fallen women. The influence of this tradition was particularly felt by the religious utopians of the Russian school of writers.

Marx's saying that religion is the opium of the people finds an unexpected application in this field. Western writers, who were little affected by the mysteries of the heavens, were locked into their intellectual systems and could find no escape for the repentant prostitute within her society. The Russians, on the other side of the enlightenment border, were still able to find enough strength in religion to administer a healing mixture to the soul and body of the repentant sinner. So the prostitute of Russian literature was not condemned beyond hope. Both Dostoevsky's Sonya and Tolstoy's Maslova find their salvation in their faith. One can easily imagine Sonya going on her beat with one hand holding an umbrella and the other on the Bible. Her reading of the Resurrection of Lazarus from St John is typical, so is her preaching of suffering as the threshold to salvation, her dream of her beloved coming to smother her foot with his tears, her present of a little cypress-wood cross to Raskolnikov before he gives himself up, and finally her redemption of Raskolnikov and restoring him to Christianity. Only through that could Dostoevsky see a salvation for the fallen and innocent Sonya.

Although *Resurrection* was a title indicative by itself of the religious tone of Tolstoy's novel, Maslova's involvement in religion is hardly noticeable. The writer was preoccupied with the guilt of her seducer, and because Tolstoy is concentrating on his salvation through religion, Maslova is able to slip quietly into her own salvation through the door of the revolutionary movement which was marching towards its final triumph in the October Revolution. This was the only salvation which could befit a girl shanghaied from the midst of a church congregation while angelic hymns rose up to the high heavens, only to be abused through her very spiritual intoxication and lose her virginity.

When the palliative of religion was withdrawn, together with the hope of socialism, the Russian harlot was left with nothing but a bleak living and a tragic death. This was the lesson given by Jennie, the atheist whore of the novelist Alexander Kuprin. In 1909, Kuprin published the novel for which he is usually known, *Yama: The Pit*,[4] which dealt with the underworld life of Yama in Southern Russia. An actor, singer and journalist, the writer shocked Russia with this crude and sensational novel, since translated into many languages. The action hardly moves out of the two-rouble establishment of Anna Markovna, where in a series of vulgarly photographic tableaux painted in gory colours the novelist introduces us to the Brechtian world of capitalist prostitution, wherein the brothel-keepers sit on the city council and the city police chiefs sit in the brothels, sabre and all, debating the sorry state of morality with their pimping partners.

Yama is one of the most pessimistic novels ever written on the subject. The only glimpse of hope in it flickers in one passage coming from the doubtful mind of Platonov, the reporter with the wisdom-invoking name. He replies to a question from Likhonin, the anarchist student:

"When it will cease, none will tell you. Perhaps when the magnificent Utopias of the socialists and anarchists will materialize, when the world will become everyone's and no one's, when love will be absolutely free and subject only to its own unlimited desires, when mankind will fuse into one happy family, wherein will perish the distinction between mine and thine and there will come a paradise upon earth, and man will again become naked, glorified and without sin."

This Russian novel is remarkably free from religious sentiments, but its writer makes the peculiar analogy between the convent life and the brothel life in which his whores have the features of nuns and a secure, secluded existence, with plenty of boredom between the services. One of the whores, Tamara, was in fact once a nun. The world outside the brothel is a dark world full of bestiality and pitfalls. Into this secure and warm house marches a group of students looking for fun. The anarchist Likhonin takes it upon himself to redeem one of the girls and begs Jennie to follow him, but Jennie has a wide-open eye and no illusions. Liubka accepts his offer, much against the advice of those around her. Platonov reminds the student of the Russian populists who married peasant girls out of principle, only to find the girls soon getting fatter and fatter through lying all day in bed eating biscuits. Nevertheless, Liubka ventures into the world of redemption and proves to have the familiar golden heart. Likhonin arranges for her an extensive educational programme extending from Marxism to literature and chemistry. Yet Liubka's past follows her and tempts another student to compromise her. Already tired of his girl, Likhonin avails himself of the opportunity to send away the innocent Liubka who, after desperate attempts to keep herself away from the brothel, is finally compelled to crawl back to her procuress and beg for forgiveness.

Kuprin has no kind opinion for anyone, from the richest bourgeois to the poorest revolutionary student. They are all vile creatures ready to use women without the slightest care for their feelings. Another mark which Likhonin's group leave behind is syphilis, which one of them gives to Jennie. Here we get the avenger prostitute as Jennie, wild with anger and unhappiness, resolves to infect all men. But Jennie is infected with the heart of gold as well; her courage fails her when she is in bed with a young and healthy cadet, and she shows him the horror in her larynx and calls for another girl to come and take her place.

Isn't she right in taking revenge? Is there any way out for her? Is there a God and another life? She asks these questions of the wise reporter, who gives her no answer – "I don't want to lie to you."

Burdened with her new sense of shame, unable to avenge herself, she hangs herself in the lavatory. Most of the girls follow a similar track, Verka and Manka are savagely killed. Tamara goes to prison for robbery, and Pasha ends up in a mental asylum.

Kuprin was one of many writers who preferred to view this problem in psychological terms, yet his grasp of psychology was partial, and he produced unconvincing characters and implausible situations. For him, prostitutes were in two categories: "They are either hysterical liars, deceivers, dissemblers, with a coolly perverted mind and a sinuous dark soul, or else undoubtedly self-denying, blindly devoted, foolish, naive animals." In one word, as he sees them, they are psychopaths. Poor Pasha was so popular because every time she had a man, her screams and groans of ecstasy were heard throughout the house until she was carried out, after a score of men, in a delirious coma. However, practically all Kuprin's whores came from the second category, the *Dame aux Camélias* category; after all "the value of the human soul may be known by the depth of its fall and the height of its flight".

Liubka's reform venture is echoed in the tender story of Aminta,[5] by the Italian writer Giovanni Comisso. The consumptive Aminta tries to escape from her doom and the exploitation of her drunkard father by running away with a violinist, who soon gets tired of her and abandons her. She is forced to retrace her steps to the streets of Siena through the valley of Fontebranda, from which the squeals of stuck pigs and the shouts of butchers rise up as they wash the blood from their hands at the slaughterhouse. The prettiest girl in Siena finally dies in her dingy cold room, on a bed hard as a rock. "Tell me if she wasn't pretty, my Aminta," says her mother as she raises the veil from the swollen earth-coloured face with the half-open mouth. "I didn't know where to go," says the fictitional narrator. "I entered the main street which was filled with people coming boldly towards me. The shop windows were full of cardboard masks, swollen, with half-opened mouths."

In Western Europe, where religion began to lose its relevance to social problems, most writers were left with only the condemnation of the prostitute – a position consolidated by the heredity theories and the concept of the *femme fatale*, which permeated French literature. Emile Zola was one victim of this school of thought, and the fatalities of the flesh became a central point in his novels, attacking and corroding his claim to scientific realism. One idea which attracted him was the biological theory that the first lover remained ever present in the mind of any woman, so much so that she would produce children who inherited his character years after his disappearance. This fatalism which often drove the woman to degrade her lover and destroy him had obsessed Zola in his early novels, particularly in *Madeleine Férat* (1868), before he turned more seriously to the social themes.[6] In *La Confession de Claude* (1865), he dealt with the hopelessness of the fallen woman in the futile attempt of the idealist Claude to reform Laurence. Indeed, the whole story reflected Zola's own experience when he lived with his first mistress, Berthe.[7]

Zola was only one in a long line of French writers who dealt with this situation. Balzac's aforementioned heroine, Esther, tries her luck with salvation. She works in a shirt manufacturing factory for twenty-eight sous a piece, and spends a whole month eating potatoes only. The master of French realism ridiculed the doomed attempt of the fallen woman to save herself. Esther, another whore born with a heart of gold, sinks again and falls into the tentacles of the scheming Lucian. For him alone did she abandon her profession, but the ruthlessness of her lover finally leads her to her inevitable doom as she takes her poison. Villiers de l'Isle-Adam wrote *The Bienfilatre Sisters*, in which one of the sisters falls in love and also tries in vain to redeem her position. Berthe, introduced to prostitution by the pimp Buba, follows the same dead-end road of hopeless salvation in *Buba de Montparnasse*, written by Charles-Louis Philippe in 1901.

Part of the trouble with this theme is the writers' inability to accept that the brothel is often by far a happier home for a poor proletarian woman than the factory of the capitalist or the kitchen of a womanizer. When all is said and examined, life in the *Yama* brothel is truly richer than in a cotton mill, and the hours under a silly old man more human than in front of a switchboard. What fool would choose Gervaise's life instead of Nana's? The outcry of *Yama*'s whores against the goody-goody German countess who comes to take them to a reformatory is one of the most realistic pieces in Kuprin's story, supported by the evidence of the reform society already alluded to above. The majority of prostitutes who drifted back to the proletarian life and domestic service every now and then discovered soon that rehabilitation was not worth their while and returned to their former life. What they used to give sensibly for money, they found themselves expected to give foolishly for nothing in the life of respectability. This simple deduction, that whoredom was better than the new factory life, was not to be accepted by the ideologists of the establishment, and other interpretations were therefore put forward – that the prostitute must be mad, or society unchristian.

The latter interpretation was embraced more commonly by the English school of reformers and Utopian socialists. In John Galsworthy's *Skin Game*, Chloe finds her salvation, after long unhappy experiences, in her marriage to Hornblower, a young upstart who buys the property of Hillcrist, who comes from an old-established family and who knows people's Christian names only from their tombstones. In vain does the young wife and former prostitute try to win the respect and kindness of her neighbours. In a touching scene with Mrs Hillcrist, she appeals to her to treat her like a human being, but the two families are already fighting a feud in which the respectable Hillcrists unscrupulously use the blackmail of Chloe's former agent. Notwithstanding Chloe's desperate efforts to avoid the disaster by offering even her own body to her old agent, the inevitable happens, her past is revealed, and the up-and-coming Hornblowers are crushed and forced to sell everything. Chloe, now rejected by her husband, rushes out into the night and commits suicide. True to life, the character seen in the harshest light in this sad play of social conflict is the ruthless Mrs Hillcrist, the "respectable" woman ever vindictive to her fallen sister.

Chloe's fault is that in her desperate search for salvation she chose not to inform her husband of her past. The heroine of *The Second Mrs Tanqueray* (1893) is a more formidable personality and keeps nothing from her loving husband, but the demons of established morality do not spare her and she too is driven to suicide. This play, a minor masterpiece of its day, drew tears from thousands of theatregoers and made the name of its writer, Sir Arthur Pinero. Paula's famous words, "I am sorry, Aubrey," said to her husband at the breaking point of all her hopes, sum up the sorry effort of the woman with a past to overcome the rejection of her society.

Where the redemption of a fallen woman was prescribed by a writer, it usually took place far away from her society, in the new or the colonial world in the case of West Europeans, and Siberia in the case of East Europeans. Whereas Sonya and Maslova are sent to Siberia, Dickens's Emily and Martha are dispatched to Australia. The fatalist Nancy (*Oliver Twist*), on the other hand, rejects the offer of Mr Brownlow to send her abroad at his expense and so save her:

> "I am chained to my old life. I loathe and hate it now, but I cannot leave it. I must have gone too far to turn back – and yet I don't know, for if you had spoken to me so, some time ago, I should have laughed it off. But this fear comes over me again. I must go home."

And home she goes, where the good woman meets her frightful end and dies praying with the blood streaming from her battered head.

Before her last parting from the Brownlows, Rose asks her what will become of her if she stays with the same gang. The prostitute points to the Thames – "It may be years hence, or it may be only months." The river, along which so many macabre scenes take place in Dickens, captured the imagination of the great novelist, like many other writers on the subject, as a symbol of fornication and corruption.

"Oh, the river! Oh, the river!" Martha goes on repeating passionately in that dismal scene at Millbank with its prison walls, the slime and mud, the sewage and decay, rank weeds and hanging chains, the rusty iron monsters of discarded steam boilers, furnaces and anchors:

> "I know it's like me! I know that I belong to it. I know that it's the natural company of such as I am! It comes from country places, where there was once no harm in it – and it creeps through the dismal streets, defiled and miserable – and it goes away, like my life, to a great sea, that is always troubled – and I feel that I must go with it! ... I can't keep away from it. I can't forget it. It haunts me day and night. It's the only thing in all the world that I am fit for, or that's fit for me. Oh, the dreadful river."

The action in *David Copperfield*, the novel which Dickens evidently dedicated to the "social evil", is kept most of the time by the edge of the water, the great symbol of sex, craving and death, by the River Thames and the English Channel, with boats, boathouses, ships and sea storms. The eternity of sex and sin becomes bound up with the eternity of the sea and its waves. In the little town of Yarmouth, Little Emily grows up in a boathouse with a seagoing family, and works in a milliner's firm. Just before her wedding, she elopes with James Steerforth, a prosperous young man, and finishes her months of love in a brothel in London. From the same firm of milliners comes Emily's workmate Martha, the "poor wurem ... as is trod under foot by all the town. Up street and down street. The mould o' the churchyard don't hold any that the folk shrink away from more."

Perhaps the black doom of the harlot and her quick progress towards a painful early death are seen in an even starker light in the story of Alice Brown (*Dombey and Son*). It is interesting to compare the Dickensian heroine with Tolstoy's Maslova. Both were born illegitimate, seduced and abandoned by influential men, driven to the dens of vice and crime, convicted and sentenced to deportation. But Miss Brown meets no revolutionaries in Australia to restore her faith in humanity, and returns to England full of bitterness and despair. That is the time when we find her urging her steps to London under howling wind and pelting rain:

> miserably dressed; the soil of many country roads in varied weather – dust, chalk, clay, gravel – clotted on her grey cloak by the streaming wet; no bonnet on her head, nothing to defend her rich black hair from the rain, but a torn handerchief; with the fluttering ends of which, and with her hair, the wind blinded her so that she often stopped to push them back, and look upon the way she was going.

Under such conditions, she is offered the hospitality of the kindly Miss Harriet Carker, the sister of her former seducer, yet unknown to her. In the course of the conversation, while the prostitute is bandaging her bleeding feet, Harriet politely suggests that her guest is, after all, repentant. "No," retorts the wandering woman, "I am not! I can't be. I am no such thing. Why should I be penitent, and all the world go free? They talk to me of my penitence. Who's penitent for the wrongs that have been done to me?" Alice was the avenger whore, and one of thousands who found their reformation a worthless dirty trick. Her life force revolved around one idea, to follow her vile seducer wherever he went and execute justice on him. But Alice was not only the avenger; she was also the prostitute with the heart of gold. Just when she has Carker at her mercy, she hurries at the eleventh hour to Harriet to give him warning and enable him to escape. Revenge and forgiveness, seemingly contradictory but actually no more than twins of the same mother – justice – and the fruit of the excessive preoccupation with right and wrong, ironically achieve their synthesis and reunion in the bosom of the whore. Yet the cruelty of the middle class is such that this forgiveness of the prostitute must remain unilateral, and the wretched Alice Brown dies in the prime of her life, serene in her agony and disease.

In *Dombey and Son*, Dickens made another frontal attack on the champions of heredity and believers in the inescapable vice of the psychopathic "type". In a far-fetched dénouement, he contrived a blood relationship between Alice and the high and mighty Mrs Dombey. Both are cousins of the first degree, but Alice falls easily to seduction, crime and venality while Edith Dombey resists the pass of even the man with whom she elopes. To make the comparison even fairer, the pass is made by the selfsame man, Carker, whom Edith had to fend off at knife-point. The difference between the two is environment: Alice was the illegitimate child brought up in misery by a poor country wench, whereas Edith was the respectable daughter brought up by well-to-do parents. To spotlight the moral even more, Alice spells it out on her deathbed:

> "I have felt, lying here, that I should like you to know this. It might explain, I have thought, something that used to help to harden me. I had heard so much, in my wrongdoing, of my neglected duty, that I took up with the belief that duty had not been done to me, and that as the seed was sown, the harvest grew. I somehow made it out that when ladies had bad homes and mothers, they went wrong in their way, too; but that their way was not so foul a one as mine, and they had need to bless God for it."

Nevertheless, something of the common blood leaves its imprint on both women in their sense of pride. Edith preserves her self-respect by rejecting the sexual demands of husbands and lovers alike; she is rich. Alice does the same by accepting the sexual demands of all men who can pay; she is poor. The alternatives open to the poor are limited and often the same – just like the food they eat and the clothes they wear. The alternatives open to Alice are to let her mother go begging in the streets and accept the alms of her former enemies, or to go out herself and sell her beauty in the market of vice. She does the latter, and fights with her mother whenever she catches her accepting alms. Her other two alternatives in Victorian England were death or the something worse than death that followed in a natural sequence.

No great writer involved himself more closely in the fate and rehabilitation of the common whore than Charles Dickens. His interest was destined to have a practical application when he came across the benefactress Baroness Burdett-Coutts. In a lengthy letter which he addressed to her on 26 May 1846,[7] he set out to explain his programme and expectations for the reform of the fallen women. Many critical judgements may be passed on Dickens's realism, but his appreciation of the position of the prostitute remains a monument to his insight and careful examination of his environment, not only in his period but also in comparison with present-day sociological knowledge on the problem, within the capitalist terms of reference. His association with Miss Coutts resulted in the setting up of the Urania Cottage in Shepherds Bush, London, which he called the Home for the Homeless Women.

The work of this institution confirms the general position already outlined. It was difficult to find women willing to accept the charitable reform offered by the house, and many of those who did come soon departed. Dickens's Urania Cottage was attested as one of the most successful homes for the reclamation of the prostitute, but it could only manage to accommodate fifty-seven women from 1847 to 1853. Of these, thirty were saved and went to Australia and the colonies, but no more than seven women managed to find husbands.[8] This was more or less the fifty-fifty chance of reclamation which Dickens anticipated in his letter. His interest began to sag from 1854 when he himself became a "fallen" man – in terms of sexual lapse – but Urania Cottage until then absorbed a great deal of his energy. His programme, based on Captain Maconnochie's system of rewarding the woman by marks for her progress and penalizing her by deducting marks according to her errors, showed an inclination towards treating the residents of the cottage as mental cases, something which he also reflected in his writing, as will be mentioned below.

The colonial reformers' movement which was active at the time recommended migration to the colonies as the best solution for the country's industrial social evils, including overpopulation, crime and immorality. Taking into consideration the unbending attitude of Victorian society towards the fallen woman *in situ*, Dickens was impressed by this approach and adopted it as part of his programme for the inmates of Urania Cottage. After a long course of teaching, religious brainwashing and penitence, they were shipped to the colonies under trusty guidance and on some orderly ships. Two years after he had embarked on this reform work, he began to write *David Copperfield* as a sermon on the subject.

When Dickens wrote *Oliver Twist* in 1838-9, there was no hope for the whore and Nancy met her doom. The dreadful scene of her death dominated the mind of her creator for years to come. Much against the advice of his doctors, he went on playing the taxing part of the murderer until he precipitated his own sad death. The fate of Nancy went on agitating Dickens's sensitive humanitarian mind throughout the eight years following his portrayal of the helpless woman, when he addressed himself attentively to the problem and hammered out his programme for her redemption.

David Copperfield (1849-50) portrayed a different type of woman. Unlike the fatalist Nancy or the tragic Alice Brown, the unhappy Martha is groping for a straw to cling to, and a straw comes her way when she is begged by Copperfield to help him find Emily. Dickens recognized the fact of being needed as a vital hub in the psychology of the whore. But the redemption of the two women could not take place in England. Emily found time to heal her wounds, and Martha a husband who accepted her past, in Australia where women – as

Dickens did not omit to mention – were in short supply. *David Copperfield* dwells on many aspects of the classic harlot's progress accepted by contemporary sociologists, but it omits the fatalistic notions about heredity, and shows no development of revenge. Dickens's harlots are too good to leave room for that. Revenge and villainy are put at the doorstep of the respectable middle class. One can well hear the advice of the master of English realism: if you have to choose between the warm-hearted, self-giving, innocent soul of the prostitute and the calculating frigid heart of the respectable lady, then by God make no mistake – take the prostitute. Emily and Martha are pointedly contrasted with Miss Rosa Dartle and Miss Jane Murdstone. Miss Murdstone, with her cold, stiff fingers, her eyebrows with which she follows people rather than see them with her eyes, with the little fetters on her wrists and round her neck worn all her life, reminding Copperfield of the fetters over a gaol door, and suggesting to all beholders what is to be expected within, keeps on appearing and reappearing in the novel to keep in sight the dismal puritanism of middle-class morality and the iced hypocrisy of its soul.

Women's cruelty to the fallen woman was expressed by the other refined lady, Miss Rosa Dartle. Green with envy and jealousy and red with rage and revenge, she does not hesitate to walk into the shady house of Martha to encounter Little Emily in her room and torment her in a melodramatic scene. Despite the wretched state of the abandoned Emily, Miss Dartle goes on taunting her through clenched teeth: "The miserable vanity of these earth-worms ... part of the trade of your home ... bought and sold like any other vendible thing your people dealt in." These were the firm women who kept even their necklaces firm on their bosoms, who treated Mrs Copperfield with firmness and sent her to the grave, who beat up her son to educate him, and kept firm hands on their purses and title deeds. They were a different species from the volatile Emily and Martha with their restless minds, fleshy hearts and moods as changeable as the sea and the ships which decorated Emily's London lodgings; thirsty for a better life and happier hours than the drudgery of a milliner's toil at four shillings a week.

To the revolutionary socialists, the idea of redeeming the prostitute, like all reforming ideas, is ridiculous. The prostitute is the product of her society, and without altering that society you stand as much chance of redeeming her as of controlling population by recommending homosexuality. She is not just a product of this society; she is its quintessence and emblem. Her position in such literature remained one of acceptance. Such is the lot of the Brechtian harlot. Only the gods themselves could manage to move one of Brecht's women to seek redemption. With the little money put by the gods into Shen Te's hand, the noble prostitute of Setzuan is asked to be good. How can she do it in this wretched world around her, she asks the gods. "You will manage," they say to her in despair, not having a head for economics themselves. Along the same futile path of the reformed prostitute, Shen Te sets out. She is exploited by everybody, made pregnant and abandoned by the man she loves, forced to borrow money on behalf of others and to face the rigours of the law.

Yet, *The Good Woman of Setzuan* was written not as another black mass for capitalism, but as a hymn of glory to socialism. Shen Te has to undergo a schizophrenic process resulting in one personality which is hard, ruthless and practical, to cope with the capitalist world around her, and another which is tender, carefree and foolishly generous, to satisfy the call of goodness within her soul. Only with the amalgamation of ruthlessness – the dictatorship of the proletariat – and humanism – the application of socialism – can the new brave world of justice redeem the prostitutes, the thieves, the beggars and the rascals who enter Shen Te's tobacco factory. In this new establishment wherein there are neither ladies nor right honourable gentlemen, neither dukes nor duchesses, neither respectable wives and industrious husbands nor bishops and moralists, Shen Te has no need to be accepted and no reason to conceal her past. Yet it is remarkable that, even in the work of Bertolt Brecht, the prostitute has to go from Europe to China to find that socialist redemption.

Unlike the emergent states of the Third World which acted as if the question of prostitution had been solved by the mere fact of gaining independence and did no more than order the police to clear the prostitutes off the streets, close their houses and ban any literature on the subject, the socialist countries made a conscious effort to rehabilitate these women and find them suitable work. Success in this cannot be described as complete. It is a problem which has many causes and facets, and unemployment and poverty – important as they are – cannot be treated as the whole question. In many East European capitals there is now a tacit acceptance and semi-official organization of prostitution indicated by police control and regular compulsory medical check-ups. This kind of reluctant arrangement will remain inadequate in the absence of a courageous admission which can then have its true expression in the arts and literature of the country. It was with some struggle that writers were able to tackle this question, and it will be a considerable loss for us to deny them now the right to treat this theme which has enriched the literature, conscience and social progress of the whole human race.

Notes

1: Prostitution in History and Literature

1. Quran, IV: 15 and XXIV: 2.
2. *Prevention of Prostitution*, League of Nations, C.26, M.26, 1943, IV, Geneva, 1943, p.26.
3. This point is discussed by Engels in his *Origin of the Family*. According to him, jealousy and pairing were developed after the disintegration of the old communistic society. Karl Marx and Frederick Engels, *Selected Works*, Vol. II (Moscow, 1959), pp. 180-94.
4. F. Henriques, *Prostitution and Society*, Vol. 1 (London, 1962), pp. 328-9.
5. ibid., pp. 26-7.
6. See C. Seltman, *Women in Antiquity* (London, 1956), p. 128.
7. T. Rattray, *Sex in History* (London, 1953), p. 229.
8. Petronius, *The Satyricon* (London, 1963), pp. 73, 81-7.
9. Deuteronomy, 23:17-18.
10. M. Weber, *Ancient Judaism* (New York, 1952), p. 237.
11. ibid., p. 237.
12. I Corinthians, 6:13-15.
13. St Cyprian, *Discipline and Habit of Virgins* (London, 1675).
14. *The Venereal Diseases*, Office of Health Economics (London, 1963).
15. Citation in F. Henriques, *Prostitution in Europe and the New World* (London, 1963), p. 91.
16. F. Henriques testifies that women have more often than not enhanced their natural qualities and physical beauty by the practice of prostitution; see *Modern Sexuality* (London, 1968), pp. 194-6.
17. Engels, *Origins of the Family*, op. cit., p. 242.
18. C. Pearl, *The Girl with the Swansdown Seat* (London, 1955), p. 53.
19. Henriques, *Prostitution in Europe*, p. 55.
20. ibid., p. 186.
21. See evidence submitted on behalf of the Church to the Wolfenden Committee, *Sexual Offenders and Social Punishment* (London, 1956).

134   The Prostitute in Progressive Literature

2: Under the Shadow of Capitalism

1. *Sexual Offences*, pp. 43-4.
2. See H. Marcuse, *Reason and Revolution* (London, 1968), p. 34.
3. Henriques, *Prostitution in Europe*, p. 143.
4. W. Acton, *Prostitution, Considered in its Moral, Social, and Sanitary Aspects in London and Other Large Cities and Garrison Towns* (London, 1870).
5. Ben L. Reitman, *The Second Oldest Profession* (London, 1936), p. 3.
6. S. O'Callaghan, *The White Slave Trade* (London, 1965).
7. Henriques, *Modern Sexuality*, p. 250.
8. *The Maiden Tribute to Modern Babylon*, Report of the *Pall Mall Gazette*'s Secret Commission, July 1885.
9. *Report of the Special Body of Experts on the Traffic in Women and Children*, 1927/C.52 M.52. 1927, IV, p. 15.
10. *Report to the Council by the Commission of Enquiry into the Traffic of Women and Children in the Far East*, 1932/C.849 M.393. 1932, IV, pp. 25, 41, 95, 469.
11. F. Harris, *Bernard Shaw* (London, 1931).
12. 4 September 1893, *Collected Letters, 1874-1897* (London, 1965).
13. ibid., 10 June 1896, p. 632.
14. Harris, op. cit., p. 180.
15. J. Ervine, *Bernard Shaw* (London, 1956), p. 253.

3: Victims of Circumstance

1. W. Acton, *Prostitution*.
2. H. Mayhew, *London Labour and the London Poor* (London, 1861), Vol. 1, p. 413.
3. *The Second Sex* (London, 1969), p. 289.
4. Dickens's Letters, 26 May 1846, Vol. 1, p. 149.
5. Quoted in H. Marcuse, *Reason and Revolution*, pp. 273f.
6. Karl Marx and Frederick Engels, *Complete Works* (London, 1975), Vol. 3, p. 306.
7. Cited in *Women and Communism*, pp. 33-4.
8. *Women and Communism*, p. 162.
9. Karl Marx and Frederick Engels, *Selected Works* (Moscow, 1951), Vol. II, p. 209.
10. ibid., pp. 212-13.
11. *Rabochaya Pravda*, 26 July 1913, cited in *Women and Communism*, pp. 40-1.
12. *Pravda*, 6 November 1919, cited in *Women and Communism*, p. 59.
13. See *Women and Communism*, pp. 92-3.
14. Text in Lenin, *Selected Works* (London, 1946), Vol. 9, p. 493.
15. W. Gallacher, *The Case for Communism* (London, 1949), p. 116.
16. G.B. Shaw, *The Intelligent Woman's Guide to Socialism and Capitalism* (London, 1937), Vol. 1, pp. 196-8.
17. G.B. Shaw, *Our Theatres in the Nineties* (London, 1932), Vol. II, p. 297.
18. G.B. Shaw's *Complete Prefaces* (London, 1965), p. 41.
19. *Complete Prefaces*, p. 36.

4: Brecht and his Underworld

1. See F. Ewen, *Bertolt Brecht* (London, 1970), p. 176.
2. Bertolt Brecht, *Plays* (London, 1960), Vol. 1, p. 183.
3. *The Threepenny Opera*.
4. M. Esslin, *Brecht, A Choice of Evils* (London, 1936), p. 128.
5. See O'Callaghan, op. cit., p. 156.
6. The income of callgirls in West Germany was estimated by the Income Tax in 1965 as £150 million per annum.
7. See Reitman, op. cit., pp. 121f.
8. O'Callaghan, op. cit.
9. Henriques, *Modern Sexuality*, pp. 14, 161.
10. ibid., pp. 15-25 and 27.
11. Cited in Ewen, op. cit., p. 185.
12. Cited in Esslin, op. cit., p. 44.
13. *Encounter*, prepared by Wayland Young, May 1959.
14. O'Callaghan, op. cit.

5: Under Colonialism

1. Henriques, *Prostitution and Society*, Vol. I, p. 169.
2. ibid., p. 375.
3. *Report to the Council by the Commission of Enquiry into the Traffic of Women and Children in the Far East*, 1932/C.849 M.393. IV, p. 65.
4. *Report to the Special Body*, C52. M52, 1927, IV.
5. O'Callaghan, op. cit., p. 65.
6. H. Mayhew, *Those That Will Not Work*, Vol. IV, p. 57.
7. ibid., pp. 125, 116.
8. E.H. Erikson, *Gandhi's Truth: On the Origins of Militant Nonviolence* (London, 1970), pp. 219-20.
9. See his pamphlet, *India: Home Rule* (Hind Swarag).
10. *Indian Short Stories* (New India Publishing Company, 1946).

6: Black Women, White Men

1. F. Henriques, *Stews and Strumpets* (London, 1961), p. 371.
2. R.A. Bone, *The Negro Novel in America* (New Haven, Conn., 1958), p. 70.
3. See Henriques, *Prostitution in Europe*, pp. 251-5.
4. See S.H. Bronz, *Roots of Negro Racial Consciousness* (New York, 1964).
5. *Report of the East African Royal Commissions* (London, 1955).
6. *Report of Central African Council, Migrant Labour* (Salisbury, 1947).
7. L. Longmore, *The Dispossessed* (London, 1959), p. 138.
8. O'Callaghan, op. cit.
9. Henriques, *Stews and Strumpets*, p. 378.
10. Ekwensi to the writer, 13 March 1973.
11. E. Palmer, *An Introduction to the African Novel* (London, 1972), p. xiii.

12. Ekwensi to the writer, 13 March 1973.

7: The Woman with the Heart of Gold

1. Guy de Maupassant was a regular visitor to brothels, contracted VD and died of syphilis.
2. Pearl, op. cit., p. 111.
3. It is interesting to note that among the few plot alterations made in *Catch My Soul*, Jack Good's rock adaptation of *Othello*, was a coloured prostitute, the mistress of Cassio, who gets arrested by Iago and falsely accused of complicity in her master's injury.
4. Quoted in Henri Troyat, *Tolstoy* (London, 1968), p. 549.
5. G. Lukacs, *Studies in European Realism* (London, 1950), p. 195.
6. "Didactic Theatre" had been the name first given to Brecht's plays before "Epic Theatre" became more common.
7. Cesar Lombroso, *Criminal Man*, summarized by Gina Lombroso (London, 1911), p. 144.
8. Bone, op. cit., p. 19.
9. W. Morris, *Selected Writings* (London, 1948), p. 59.

8: The Eternal Shadow of the Warrior

1. Henriques, *Prostitution in Europe*, London, 1963, p. 42.
2. ibid., p. 55.
3. Henriques, *Modern Sexuality*, p. 61.
4. ibid., p. 238
5. Command Paper C-7148, 1893, p. XXXII.
6. Henriques, *Modern Sexuality*, p. 293-4.
7. Document no. 052C for 1927, Vol. 4, p. 13.
8. Hemmings, p. 70.

9: The Avenger and her Problem

1. W. Leck, *History of European Morals* (London, 1869).
2. Henriques, *Modern Sexuality*, p. 281.
3. A great deal has been written in attempts to psychoanalyse Zola's preoccupation with sex and fornication. See F.W. Hemmings, *Emile Zola* (London, 1966), p. 149.
4. Zola was a close friend and admirer of Cezanne.
5. Hemmings, op. cit., p. 59.
6. Greenweld, *The Call Girl* (New York, 1958).
7. Troyat, op. cit., p. 460.
8. Pearl, op. cit., p. 65.
9. H. Mayhew, op. cit., Vol. 1, p.1.
10. Troyat, op. cit., p. 326.
11. *The Times*, 16 October 1858.

12. W. Acton, pp. 3, 39.
13. Mayhew, op. cit., p. 234.
14. *Traffic in Women and Children*, 1937/C. 476 M.318, 1937, IV, p. 80.
15. W. Acton, *A Practical Treatise on the Diseases of the Urinary and Genitive Organs* (London, 1851), p. 21.
16. Acton, *Prostitution*, p. 31.
17. ibid., p. 4.
18. *Report of the Committee on Homosexual Offences and Prostitution* Cmnd. 247 (London, 1957), p. 80.
19. M. Seymour-Smith, *Fallen Women* (London, 1971), pp. 159, 197-8.
20. Henriques, *Prostitution in Europe*, p. 65.

10: Redemption

1. Henriques, *Prostitution in Europe*, pp. 183-4.
2. Henriques, *Modern Sexuality*, p. 54.
3. Acton, *Prostitution*, p. 52.
4. Hamish Hamilton, London, 1930.
5. *Great Italian Short Stories*, New York, 1959.
6. See J.C. Lapp, *Zola Before the Rougon-Macquart* (Toronto, 1964), pp. 121f.
7. Hemmings, op. cit., p. 17.
8. Walter Dexter (ed.), *Letters of Charles Dickens* (London, 1938), vol. 1, p. 749.
9. P. Collins, *Dickens and Crime* (London, 1962), p. 110. Dickens's work in connection with the reform of the prostitute is outlined on pp. 94-116 of Collins's book.

Index

Abbas, Ahmad, 73
Aberdeen, Scotland, 22
abortion, 32
Achurch, Janet, 38
adultery, 16, 48
Afra, St, 26
Africa, 33, 63-4, 65, 74, 76-84
African literature, 64, 77-84
Aidoo, Ama Ata, 80-81
Alexandria, Egypt, 34, 64, 101
Algeria, 34, 64, 68, 101
alienation, Hegelian concept of, 28, 45
Al-Sayyab, Badr Shakir, 71-2, 101
Al-Sukkaria (Mahfuz), 70
Al-Ulum, Bahr, 10
Alva, Duke of, 100
America, United States of, 17, 18, 26, 32, 33, 34, 39, 54, 56, 94, 100, 101, 115
"Aminta" (Comisso), 101, 123
Anthony, 19
Aphrodite, 18
Arab literature, 19, 71
Aretino, Pietro, 22, 23
Argentina, 34
Aristotle, 87
Armenia, 18
artists, prostitutes as subject matter of, 13, 103
As, L' (Ovettar), 68
Asia, Central, 22
Assommoir, L' (Zola), 110, 112
Assyria, 18
Athens, Greece, 18, 19

Attaway, William, 32
Augustine, 25
Augustus, Emperor, 19
Australia, 125, 129

Baalbek, Lebanon, 18
Babylonia, 21
Baghdad, Iraq, 10
Balcony, The (Genet), 81, 101, 108-9
"Ballad of Sexual Submissiveness" (Brecht), 56
"Ballad of the Pimp" (Brecht), 56
Balzac, Honoré de, 24, 27-8, 87, 124
Banjo (McKay), 75
Barclay Perkins, 57
Basisu, Mu'in, 72
"Bastard Reared by the British and the Americans, The" (Nasir), 66-7
Basutoland, 76
Battle of Algiers, The (Pontecorvo), 65
Bayn al-Qasrain (Mahfuz), 68
Bebel, August, 34
Beira, Mozambique, 77
Beirut, Lebanon, 33, 34, 64
Belgium, 33
Bentley's Miscellany, 96
Ben Yena, Professor Amitay, 64-5
Berkely, Mrs, 33, 61
Berlin, Germany, 53, 59
Berliner Requiem (Brecht), 55
Bible, 8

Index

Bienfilatre Sisters, The (De l'Isle Adam), 124
Black literature, 32, 75-6, 79-84, 95-6
Black women, 74-84
"Blind Prostitute, The" (Al-Sayyab), 71-2
Bloch, Iwan, 22, 116
Blood on the Forge (Attaway), 32
Boccaccio, Giovanni, 25
Book of Songs, The, 19
Bordeaux, France, 33
"Boule de Suif" (Maupassant), 34, 85-6, 94, 101
Brecht, Bertolt, 16, 24, 34, 39, 52-6, 68, 87, 91-3, 97-8, 105, 112, 114, 131
"Bridge of Sighs, The" (Hood), 55
Bright, R. Golding, 38
Britain, 54, 57, 115, 117
"Brothel, The" (Al-Sayyab), 72
Brothers Karamazov, The (Dostoevsky), 110
Brussels, Belgium, 36
Buba de Montparnasse (Philippe), 124
Budapest, Hungary, 36
Buñuel, Luis, 92
Burdett-Coutts, Baroness, 128

Cairo, Egypt, 34, 40, 72, 73
Candy (Southern), 94
Capital (Marx), 8, 45, 46
capitalism, 7, 15-16, 24, 39, 45-6, 48, 49, 50, 52, 58, 62, 131
Caribbean literature, 75
Carthage, 21
Catch 22 (Heller), 103, 104-7
Caucasian Chalk Circle, The (Brecht), 98
"Change of Partners" (Schnitzler), 102
Chekhov, Anton, 90
China, 19, 34, 37, 79, 131
Chios, 18
Christ, 21, 25, 44, 120
Christianity, 7, 11, 20, 21, 26, 75, 117, 120-21
Cinyras, King, 18
Cleopatra, 19
Comisso, Giovanni, 101, 123
communism, 46
Communist Manifesto (Marx and Engels), 10, 58
Condition of the Working Classes in England (Engels), 46-7
Confession de Claude, La (Zola), 124
Confidential Clerk, A (Eliot), 39
Congo, French, 18
contraception, 32
Conversion of England, The, 50
Corinthians, 21
Crime and Punishment (Dostoevsky), 87
Cry, the Beloved Country (Paton), 77-8
"Cutting of a Drink, The" (Aidoo), 81
Cyprian, St, 21
Cyprus, 18

Daily Chronicle, 35
Dame aux Camélias, La (Dumas), 49, 71, 86-7, 123
Darwin, Charles, 96
Daumier, Honoré, 85
David Copperfield (Dickens), 113, 126, 129-30
De Beauvoir, Simone, 42-3
Decalogue, 20
Dekker, Thomas, 120
De la Bretonne, Rétif, 114
De l'Isle-Adam, Villiers, 124
Dispossed, The (Longmore), 76
Dickens, Charles, 28-30, 41, 45, 82, 87, 88, 95, 96, 113, 125-30
dicteria, 19
Dix, Otto, 53
Dombey and Son (Dickens), 29-30, 126-8
Dostoevsky, Fyodor, 10, 25, 34, 41, 87-90, 92, 109, 110, 114, 121

drink and prostitution, 57-8
Dublin, Ireland, 103
Duel, The (Kuprin), 102
Dumas, Alexandre, 71, 86-7, 93
Duplessis, Marie, 42

Earth Spirit (Wedekind), 31
Edinburgh, Scotland, 22, 32
Egypt, 17, 21, 68, 69, 73, 100-101
Ekwensi, Cyprian, 82-4
Elagabalus, Emperor, 20
Eliot, George, 87
Eliot, T.S., 39
Engels, Frederick, 23-4, 46-7, 58
England, 18, 31, 36, 44, 67, 73, 87, 104, 112, 128, 129
Epic of Gilgamesh, 13-15, 26
Ervine, Sir John, 39
Eskimos, 17
Esslin, Martin, 56
Europe, 26, 33, 34, 50, 63, 74, 109, 123, 131
Ewen, 59

Fanny Hill, 31
Far East, 34, 64
Farman, Ghaib Tu'ama, 72-3
Five Voices (Farman), 72-3
Forsyte Saga, The (Galsworthy), 23, 87
"For Whom Things Did Not Change" (Aidoo), 80
France, 18, 19, 22, 33, 46, 85, 86, 95, 99, 101, 102, 112, 114, 116
French literature, 27, 47, 123, 124
Freud, Sigmund, 48

Gallacher, William, 49
Galsworthy, John, 23, 41, 87, 125
Gandhi, Mahatma, 66
Geishas, 19
Genet, Jean, 81, 101, 108-9
German literature, 47, 56
Germany, 16, 22, 58, 60-61, 93, 95, 102, 103
Getting Married (Shaw), 50

Ghana, 63, 80, 82
Gilgamesh, 13-15, 26
Gladstone, W.E., 9
Good Soldier Schweik (Hasek), 105
Good Woman of Setzuan, The (Brecht), 60, 92-3, 114, 131
Gorky, Maxim, 94, 96-7
Greece, 18, 19
Grosz, George, 53

Hamburg, Germany, 95
Hardy, Thomas, 43-4, 45
"Harlem Shadows" (McKay), 75-6
Harlot's Progress, A (Balzac), 27-8
Harlot's Progress, A (Hogarth), 22
Harris, Frank, 38
Hasek, Jaroslav, 105
Hegel, G.W.F., 28, 45
Heliopolis, Greece, 18
Heller, Joseph, 103, 104-7
Henriques, F., 17, 25, 112, 117, 120
hetaerae, 19, 23, 69
"Hindu Grhastha" (Sarma), 67
History of Prostitution (Sanger), 116
Hitler, Adolf, 58
Hobson, Harold, 109
Hogarth, William, 22
Holland, 33, 100
"Home to Harlem" (McKay), 75
homosexuality, 31
Honest Whore, The (Dekker), 120
Hong Kong, 34, 64
Hood, Thomas, 55
Hosea, 7
"Human Requirements and Division of Labour" (Marx), 45

Idiot, The (Dostoevsky), 10, 110
illegitimacy, 95-8
imperialism, 63
incest, 39
Independent Benevolent Association, 33

Index

India, 17, 18, 34, 63, 64, 66, 79, 100, 116
Indian literature, 67, 73
industrialization, 31-2, 61, 114, 115
Intelligent Woman's Guide to Socialism and Capitalism (Shaw), 49
Iraq, 10, 34
Iraqi literature, 71-2
Ireland, 100, 103-4
Isaiah, 7
Islam, 16, 19, 22
Israel, 64
Israeli literature, 9-10
Italy, 25, 95, 101

Jagua Nana (Ekwensi), 82-4
Jakobsen, J.P., 30-31
Japan, 15, 18
Jaria, 19
Jeffries, Mrs, 33
Jerome, St, 22
Jesus as Seen by His Friends (Kenan), 9
Judaism, 7, 20-21
Justinian, Emperor, 120

Kallachia, 10
Kama Sutra, 63
Kenan, Amos, 9
King Lear (Shakespeare), 95
Kuprin, Alexander, 102, 121-3, 124

Lagos, Nigeria, 84
Latin America, 34
Layard, Austen Henry, 13
League of Nations, 33, 34, 64, 101, 115
Lebanon, 18
Leck, W., 108
Lenin, V.I., 20, 48-9
Lewes, George Henry, 87
Libya, 60
Lombroso, Cesar, 95, 114
London, England, 31, 32, 33, 35, 42, 47, 87, 109, 114, 128

London Labour and the London Poor (Mayhew), 116
Longmore, L., 76
Louis IX, 22, 99
Lower Depths, The (Gorky), 94
Lukacs, George, 91
Lulu (Wedekind), 31, 40, 41, 101

Macao, China, 34, 64
McKay, Claude, 75-6
Maconocchie, Captain, 129
"Madame Tellier's Establishment" (Maupassant), 62
Madeleine Férat (Zola), 124
Mahfuz, Najib, 68-71, 101
Malaya, 34
male prostitution, 17
Man and Superman (Shaw), 50
Mandeville, Bernard de, 114
Maria, or the Wrongs of Women (Wollstonecraft), 41
marriage, 21, 28, 47-8, 50, 63, 86
Married Life of Fair Imperia (Balzac), 87
Marx, Karl, 45-6, 47, 60, 92, 120
Mary Magdalene, 25, 97, 120
Mary of Egypt, St, 26
Maupassant, Guy de, 34, 35-6, 62, 85, 101, 102, 111, 114
Mayhew, Henry, 42, 65, 114, 115, 116
Mesopotamian literature, 13-15
Meux & Co., 57-8
Mexico, 101
Middle East, 17-18, 19, 34, 64, 70, 100
Minsk, Russia, 25
missionaries, 77
Modest Defence of Public Stews (Mandeville), 114
monogamy, 17, 48, 49
Morocco, 64
Morris, William, 96
Mozambique, 77
Mrs Warren's Profession (Shaw), 36-9, 52, 96, 119

mulattos, 75, 95-6
Munich, Germany, 53
Muria community, India, 17
Muslims, 7, 22
Mylitta, 18
My Secret Life, 31

Nana (Zola), 23, 24, 34, 41, 82, 94, 95, 102, 109-13, 114, 124
Napoleon III, 102
Nasir, Kamal, 66
Nazis (National Socialists), 58, 60-61
Netherlands Indies Army, 115
News from Nowhere (Morris), 96
New York, USA, 32, 57, 61
New Zealand, 65
Nicholas Nickleby (Dickens), 28-9
Nigeria, 82-3
"Nilushka" (Gorky), 96-7

O'Callaghan, S., 33, 64, 77
O'Casey, Sean, 103-4
Oculi, Okello, 79-80
Oliver Twist (Dickens), 95, 96, 125-6, 129
Origin of the Family (Engels), 47
Ostend, Belgium, 36
Ouled Naïl, Algeria, 18
Ovettar, Taher, 68

Palestine, 20
Pall Mall Gazette, 33, 57
Palmer, Eustace, 84
Pandora's Box (Wedekind), 31
Parent-Duchatelet, 41-2
Paris, France, 32, 33, 60, 116
Paton, Alan, 77-8
Paul, St, 21
p'Bitek, Okot, 81-2
Pelagia, St, 26
perversions, 31, 33, 61
Petrashevski group, 87
Petronius, 20
Phallos, 18
Philanderer, The (Shaw), 38

Philippe, Charles-Louis, 124
Phryne, 18
Pinero, Arthur, 125
Pit, The (Kuprin). See *Yama*
Plomer, William, 78-9
Plough and the Stars, The (O'Casey), 103-4
Polgar, Alfred, 61
polygamy, 63, 74
Polynesia, 63
Pornographe, La (De la Bretonne), 114
Port Said, Egypt, 34
Pot-Bouille (Zola), 30, 109
poverty and prostitution, 49-51, 117
Prostitute, The (Oculi), 79-80
Prostitution (Acton), 116
Prostitution, Die (Bloch), 116
Puntila and his Servant, Matti (Brecht), 24, 60, 62, 68
Puritans, 24, 25

Qaddafi, Colonel, 73
qadishas, 20
Qasr al-Shawq (Mahfuz), 69
Qayna, 19

Rabelais, François, 27
"Radha" (Abbas), 73
Reitman, Ben L., 7, 33
religion and prostitution, 7, 8, 14, 15, 16, 25-6, 27, 49-50, 77, 120-21
Respectable Prostitute, The (Sartre), 94, 114
Resurrection (Tolstoy), 89-92, 110, 121
Rhodesia, 64
Rise and Fall of the City of Mahagonny, The (Brecht), 58-61
Road to Socialism (Engels), 58
Roman Empire, 19
Rousseau, Jean-Jacques, 114
Russell, Bertrand, 27

Index

Russia, 20, 25, 41, 48-9, 57, 85, 87, 91, 115, 120-21

Saigon, Vietnam, 34, 64, 65, 100
St Petersburg, Russia, 32, 87
Sanger, William W., 116
Sarma, Lajjaram, 67
Sartre, Jean-Paul, 87, 94, 114
Satyricon (Petronius), 20
Schnitzler, Arthur, 102
Scouts, Miss, 45
Second Mrs Tanqueray, The (Pinero), 125
Senghor, Léopold, 66
Seven Deadly Sins, The (Brecht), 60
sexual taboos, 17
Seymour-Smith, Martin, 117
Shakespeare, William, 7, 9, 93, 95
Shaw, George Bernard, 34, 35-9, 49-50, 52, 53, 96, 113, 114, 119-20
"Shops and their Tenants" (Dickens), 41
Siam, 34
Singapore, 64
Singh, Iqbal, 67
Skin Game (Galsworthy), 43, 125
slavery, 74-5
Smith, George, 13
Society for Juvenile Prostitution, 119
Society of Biblical Archaeology, 13
Solon, 19
"Something to Talk About on the Way to the Funeral" (Aidoo), 80
"Song of Malaya" (p'Bitek), 81-2
Southern, Terry, 94
Sparta, 17, 18
Splendeurs et Misères des Courtisanes (Balzac), 27-8
Sternberg, Fritz, 58
Street Offences Committee, 116
Stubbs, Philip, 25
suicide, prostitutes and, 8, 55
Sunday Times, 109

Tangiers, Morocco, 64
Tanzania, 64
temple harlotry, 14, 15, 17
Tess of the D'Urbervilles (Hardy), 43-4
Theodatea, St, 26
Theodora, 120
Thief and the Dogs, The (Mahfuz), 70
Threepenny Opera, The (Brecht), 52, 53-5, 56, 58, 59, 60
Tolstoy, L., 34, 87, 88-92, 95, 109, 110, 113, 114, 121, 126
Tragedy of Che Guevara, The (Basisu), 72
Trimalchio, 20
Tripoli, Libya, 34
Tunisia, 64
Turbot Wolfe (Plomer), 78-9

Utopian writers, 85, 87, 120, 125

Velázquez, 85
venereal disease, 22, 49, 100, 102, 113, 115, 116
Venice, Italy, 23
Verdi, Giuseppe, 86
Vienna, Austria, 36
Vietnam, 65, 73, 100
Viridiana (Buñuel), 93
"Vom Ertrunkenen Mädchen" (Brecht), 55

Walkly, Mary Anne, 46
War and Peace (Tolstoy), 95
war and prostitution, 16, 64-5, 66, 68-9, 99-107
Waring, James, 27
Warsaw, Poland, 25
Webb, Beatrice, 35-6
Weber, Max, 20
Wedekind, Frank, 31, 39-40, 41
Weill, Kurt, 54, 59, 60, 61
Weimar Republic, 52
"When One Is In It" (Singh), 67
Whitbread, 57

Widowers' Houses (Shaw), 37, 38
Wilson, Harold, 57
Wilson, Mary, 33
Winchester, Bishop of, 25
Wollstonecraft, Mary, 41
Women and Socialism (Bebel), 34

Yama: The Pit (Kuprin), 102, 121-3, 124
"Yvette" (Maupassant), 35, 111

Zola, Emile, 7, 9, 23, 24, 30, 34, 41, 45, 82, 90, 95, 102, 109, 110-13, 123-4